THE MONOCLED MUTINEER

ALSO BY ALAN BLEASDALE

Novels
Scully
Who's Been Sleeping in My Bed?

Scripts
Boys From the Blackstuff
Are You Lonesome Tonight?
No Surrender
Having A Ball
It's A Madhouse

THE MONOCLED MUTINEER

ALAN BLEASDALE

Adapted from the book by
William Allison and John Fairley

HUTCHINSON
London Auckland Melbourne Johannesburg

First published in 1986 by Century Hutchinson Ltd
Brookmount House, 62–65 Chandos Place, Covent Garden,
London WC2N 4NW

Century Hutchinson Publishing Group (Australia) Pty Ltd
16–22 Church Street, Hawthorn, Melbourne, Victoria 3122

Century Hutchinson Group (NZ) Ltd
32–34 View Road, PO Box 40-086, Glenfield, Auckland, 10

Century Hutchinson Group (SA) Pty Ltd
PO Box 337, Bergvlei 2012, South Africa

Set in Linotron Ehrhardt by
Rowland Phototypesetting Ltd
Bury St Edmunds, Suffolk

Printed and bound in Great Britain by
The Guernsey Press Co. Ltd., Guernsey, Channel Islands

ISBN 0 09 107340 1

The author and publishers thank the following copyright holders
for permission to reproduce the following songs:

CONTENTS

These scripts are dedicated to George Bleasdale who died a prisoner of war in France during the Spring of 1917, three months before his tenth child, my father, was born.

Alan Bleasdale

CAST

PERCY TOPLIS	Paul McGann
ANNIE WEBSTER	Jane Wood
FRANK WEBSTER	Dave Hill
JOHNSON	Malcolm Terris
TODD	Bert Parnaby
COCKNEY	Dorian Healy
GEORDIE	Billy Fellows
CRUIKSHANK	Nick Reding
MRS CRUIKSHANK	Rowena Cooper
LADY ANGELA FORBES	Penelope Wilton
STRACHEN	Ron Donachie
GENERAL THOMSON	Timothy West
FRANNY	Jerome Flynn
GILZEAN	Patrick Doyle
GENERAL ASSER	David Allister
AUSTRALIAN GAS MASK	Geoff Morrell
SCOTS GAS MASK	Louis Mellis
CHARLES STRANGE	Matthew Marsh
WOODHALL	Philip McGouch
DOROTHY	Cherie Lunghi
MAM	Paola Dionisotti
TURNER	Philip Martin Brown
FALLOWS	Aran Bell

PRODUCTION CREDITS

Location Managers	JACINTA PEEL ALAN CHARLESWORTH
First Assistant Director	MATTHEW KUIPERS
Costume Designer	CHARLOTTE HOLDICH
Make-Up Designer	DAPHNE CROKER
Sound Recordist	ROGER LONG
Associate Producer	PETER WOLFES

Film Editors	JOHN STOTHART
	JULIAN MILLER
	TARIQ ANWAR
Music	GEORGE FENTON
Photography	ANDREW DUNN
Production Designer	CHRIS ROBILLIARD
Producer	RICHARD BROKE
Director	JIM O'BRIEN

August 31, 1986 BBC

EPISODE 1
THE MAKING OF A HERO

1/1. THE SUMMER OF 1908. COURTROOM MANSFIELD PETTY SESSIONS. DAY

[*A hot day. Almost at a grateful end. We see the bleak trappings of a Magistrates' Courtroom built perhaps eighty years before.*

We also see Dickensian remnants in the faces and appearance of the Magistrates' bench and their customers.

Three men preside at a high table, the chairman, SAUNDERS, *and his colleagues in crime.*

They are inevitably middle class and affluent, and hot in their tight white collars, wishing to be elsewhere.

The Clerk of the Court is near the Magistrates' table, sitting at a desk below and in front of them.

To the right is a witness box, to the left, the holding dock. The holding dock, from a distance, seems to hold nobody but a policeman.

Subsequent benches reveal the few witnesses and members of the public.

The two uniformed policemen giving evidence are also on the benches. There are policemen at the back of the holding dock by a door leading out of the court.

The three Magistrates move out of their huddle and face forward. The bibulous SAUNDERS *looks to his fellow Magistrates, looks up and leans forward for his preamble and passing of sentence. At first he addresses everyone except the defendant in the dock*]

SAUNDERS: It has been clearly established that on the fifth day of May, in this year of Our Lord 1908, the defendant, Francis Percy Toplis, a juvenile of Sutton In Ashfield, did affect, with low cunning but little foresight of the consequences, to steal two suits of clothing. Suitably attired in one suit of clothing, suggesting a station and a class to which he did not belong, he did pledge the other suit to a pawnbroker for five shillings. Guilt is reluctantly admitted by the defendant.

[SAUNDERS *finally looks towards the defendant – and doesn't like what he sees. He bangs his gavel hard on the table*]

Stand up straight, boy. Up! *Up!*

[*We see the holding dock – and the defendant in the dock. We see only the top of his head from the hairline up.*

As SAUNDERS *shouts, we see* TOPLIS *'Stand up straight', rising another two or three inches so that his eyes appear over the edge of the dock, he stares out unblinking with a coldness and contempt*]

2A/1. INT. BIRCHING ROOM

[TOPLIS *is made to enter the room. It is bare, and humid, sunlight perhaps flooding through windows high on the wall.*

We see two big sweating policemen, one of them a sergeant. There is a birching table to which has been secured four iron clamps, two on the legs and two at the top corners. Leather straps run through the stanchions.

The men in the room look tired and bored, as if they have been doing this all day. They have.

As SAUNDERS, *in voice over, passes sentence, one of the men in the room takes a chitty off one of the escorting policemen.*

The escorts leave]

SAUNDERS (V.O.): This is not young Master Toplis's first appearance in court. Furthermore, his schoolteacher testifies merely to the boy's confidence, arrogance, and the dubious quality of ill-advised leadership. We have learnt that he is not known in Sunday School. Nevertheless, we must acknowledge that his father has left the marital home, that his mother, if I may be so bold, has contributed little to the boy's upbringing, and I suggest, Mrs Toplis, that there has been considerable, nay disgraceful, laxity on your behalf to allow a boy to have got out of control at eleven years of age . . . and so, and after due deliberation, we have determined that punishment will be somewhat more lenient than could be prescribed.

[*Pause*]

Francis Percy Toplis, this court orders that you receive six strokes of the birch and two days' imprisonment.

[*A bang on the gavel*]

STRAPPER [*to* TOPLIS]: There.

[*One of the policemen left in the room indicates that* TOPLIS *should move to the table, but* TOPLIS *remains still. The policeman pushes* TOPLIS *hard towards the table and ties* TOPLIS*'s ankles.* TOPLIS *undoes his trousers and long johns and pulls them down.* STRAPPER *pushes* TOPLIS *onto the table. The other policeman starts to tie* TOPLIS *to the table by the wrists. The leather straps hang loose. The policeman sighs as he kneels. The second policeman, at the corner of the room, lifts from a bucket a bundle of birch twigs, the top two feet of which are bound by string to form a handle. As he waits, he casually makes imaginary cricket strokes with it*]

STRAPPER [*finally*]: Are you ready?

[*No reply*]

STRAPPER: Lay on, Sir!

[*We see the beating, by the policeman with aspirations to being a modern-day W. G. Grace.* TOPLIS *makes no sound throughout. The policeman starts grunting after the fourth stroke. Upon completion, the policeman who has given the thrashing throws the birch in the bucket. It lands expertly straight into the bucket*]

3/1. INT. CORRIDOR AND CELL. DAY

[*The policemen approach carrying* TOPLIS *by the top of his arms, his legs dragging behind.*

They take him into a gloomy empty cell, and approach a low wooden bench.

They lift him, with sudden gentleness, onto the bench, so that he is lying stomach first on the bench]

THRASHER [*cheerfully*]: There you are, son. Take it easy now.

STRAPPER: And whatever you do, don't attempt to sit down.

THRASHER [*laughing*]: For a couple of days at least.

[*They turn away, go to the cell door and lock it shut.* TOPLIS *lies still. We follow the men as they walk down the corridor leading from the cells. We hear a single angry cry of pain from the cell. One of the policemen looks back towards it. Then looks again. The other policeman walks on a while, then stops and looks around towards the cell, then towards the other policeman. Then they both stare at the cell. From their point of view we see* TOPLIS *in the cell. We see him in the shadows sitting on the board facing them. We move *closer. We see the pain and determination on* TOPLIS*'s face as we get nearer and nearer, till all we see is his face and his eyes blazing out in total defiance*]

4/1. EXT. BLACKWELL PIT. DUSK AUTUMN 1910

[*It could be dawn or dusk – it is dusk.*

We see some miners, including FRANK WEBSTER, *walking away from the pit gates, up the hill towards the tight little houses.*

A Hovis atmosphere]

5/1. INT. WEBSTER'S HOUSE. DUSK

[*We see the interior of the* WEBSTERS' *one-up-and-one-down terrace in the shadow of the Blackwell Pit.*

We see ANNIE WEBSTER, *a lady in her late thirties, looking ten years older, at the kitchen sink pouring water into a jug. She comes into the living room with the jug and a kettle.*

We see TOPLIS *sitting by the fire, dressed for work*]

ANNIE: Thou has'na' slept?
TOPLIS: I noticed.

[*He smiles at her as she goes back to the kitchen. She returns with a tin bath*]

ANNIE: How can thou work nights if thee does na' sleep during the day?
TOPLIS: Ah, it's a mystery to me.
ANNIE: Percy. For God's sake, son, you'll –
TOPLIS: Yes . . . 'mother'?
ANNIE: Now your uncle and me –
TOPLIS: Don't worry. I'm going now.
ANNIE: Aye, but where?

[TOPLIS *smiles disarmingly at Annie, looks towards the door.* FRANK WEBSTER *enters after twelve hours on the day shift; walks past* TOPLIS]

FRANK: Eh y'late. Come on. Johnson's walkin' up an' down cursin'. How many times do you have to upset the man?

[TOPLIS *gets up and puts on his jacket.* FRANK *sits and takes off his.*]

TOPLIS: There speaks the king of the Miners' Federation. The very man who starts every sentence with . . . [*mimics*] . . . 'bugger the bosses'.

FRANK: Aye. Well I work hard so I'm entitled. You do sweet FA.

[*No reply*]

FRANK: You're an idle frigger. Go on, get out of it and get to work.

[TOPLIS *jokingly goes to hit* FRANK *over the head with his snap tin, behind* FRANK*'s back.* FRANK *starts taking his boots off.* TOPLIS *leaves*]

FRANK: He can charm ye all he wants, Annie, but that sod makes me sick.

ANNIE: He's my brother's son, Frank.

FRANK: Aye, happen that ought to worry you even more.

[ANNIE *goes to pick up the kettle.* FRANK *continues to take off his boots*]

6/1. INT. BLACKWELL MINERS' SOCIAL CLUB THE SAME EVENING

[*Men only. Even the barmaids.*

Many men sitting quietly drinking; dominoes; the occasional table. Men are talking with passion of the preparations for strike action. The focus of their conversation seems to be far more about the lack of safety in the pits, rather than money.

And we come to PERCY TOPLIS *seated at a rickety piano playing a simple song*]

TOPLIS: Oh, oh Antonio, he's gone away
Left me alone-io, all on my – all on my own-io,
I want to meet him with his new sweetheart
Then up will go Antonio, in his ice cream –

[*A hand comes into vision, closes the piano lid trapping* TOPLIS*'s hands. He turns to face a bull of a man,* JOHNSON, *the pit under-manager. Alongside him is the barely smaller but fatter manager of the pit,* MR TODD. *They stand there looking like Desperate Dan and Stan Laurel.* TOPLIS *doesn't flicker*]

JOHNSON: What is thou doing here?

TOPLIS: I er . . .

JOHNSON: Thou art a blacksmith, not a piano player.

TOPLIS: At last you've admitted it, Mr Johnson.

JOHNSON: *An apprentice blacksmith.*
TOPLIS: A humble start but –

[JOHNSON *picks* TOPLIS *up by the scruff of his coat*]

JOHNSON: We're two hours into the shift. Two hours! There's horses screaming down there, lad.

[JOHNSON *drags him across the club towards the door.* TODD *follows*]

7/1. EXT. PIT VILLAGE AND PIT. NIGHT

[*We see* TOPLIS *being pushed down the steps of the social club. He lands on the ground.*

TOPLIS *picks himself up as* TODD *and* JOHNSON *approach*]

TODD: Thou'll get down that shaft, and thou'll get them ponies sorted out, and I'll see you at first light.
TOPLIS: Thank you, Mr Todd, such a rare treat to speak in person with the manager of –

[JOHNSON *drags* TOPLIS *off down the street,* TODD *following behind. We then see them approaching the colliery where* JOHNSON *knocks* TOPLIS *to the ground again. As he gets to his feet he is hurled down the hill, closely followed by the two men.* JOHNSON *kicks out at him as they go, and he goes rolling down till he gets to his feet, and is immediately grabbed again*]

JOHNSON: Thou were a favour, tha' understand, tha's here as a favour to tha' uncle, to keep him quiet, the Federation prat. Who was to know it'd be thee who'd make the noise?

[JOHNSON *sends* TOPLIS *flying again. He is knocked against the gate post of the pit and lies still this time.* TODD *and* JOHNSON *crouch down beside him. We fade as the two men pump spurts of water over* TOPLIS*'s head and shoulders*]

8/1. EXT. PIT SHAFT AND COLLIERY THE NEXT MORNING

[*We see* TOPLIS *with the other men in the cage coming up from the pit shaft.*

Small, stunted black and tired men standing in silence. They move towards the light of day.

TOPLIS *alone.*

We see them passing level with the windows of the manager's office, where TODD *and* JOHNSON *are at the windows, watching.*

TOPLIS *goes straight past and on towards the gates.*

TODD *knocks on the window pane.*

One of the miners looks around, hesitantly stops.

JOHNSON *comes to the door. Bellows*]

JOHNSON: Toplis. Toplis!

[*The men carry on walking; so does* TOPLIS]

JOHNSON: Toplis! . . . Don't come back then, Toplis. Keep going and don't come back . . . Tha'll never get another job around here. I'll make sure of that!

[*We see* TOPLIS *walking away quietly, quickening his pace. He throws his bottle and snap tin away and gives his lamp to one of the miners*]

9/1. INT. WEBSTER'S LIVING ROOM NIGHT

[*We see* FRANK *sitting in front of the tin bath in front of the fire.* ANNIE *is fetching the water from the stove*]

FRANK: . . . Good. I'm glad.

ANNIE: Is that all?

FRANK: No, it's not. Tha'll be glad too. Tha'll be glad tha' maiden name's Toplis and tha' married name's Webster, tha'll be glad he's causin' trouble in some other town, and tha'll be glad if he never comes back. And that's the end of it.

[ANNIE *lifts the kettle, pours water into the jug and pours the water over* FRANK*'s neck*]

ANNIE: . . . He took five shillings.

FRANK [*determined*]: That's only to be expected, I suppose.

ANNIE: And tha' bike.

FRANK [*clenching*]: What?

ANNIE: . . . And tha' suit's gone missing, Frank.

[FRANK *stands up. He starts to grab his clothes and get dressed as he rages*]

FRANK: I'll break every bone in his bloody body! I'll kick him to Mansfield and back, I will, so help me . . . How long's he been gone? Is George Meredith's bike fixed yet, Annie, is it? Which way did he go?

[*Looks at* ANNIE]

Where's my boots, Annie?

10/1. YOUNG TOPLIS MONTAGE

[*We see in close up* TOPLIS *at a window sill, casually.*

We see an attractive older girl looking out at him from the open window.

They are both giggling and whispering.

The girl looks beyond him out of the window.

TOPLIS *affects a languid mock surprise. We move away to see some people looking up at* TOPLIS *who is standing on a drainpipe, one floor up*]

10B/1. EXT. A COUNTRY LANE, ON A HILL

[*A motor car.*

A couple in the field below are enjoying a splendid picnic.

We see TOPLIS, *with suitcase, watching the couple, then approaching the car, and throwing in his suitcase.*

As discreetly as possible he attempts to crank-start the car]

10C/1. EXT. TOPLIS IN THE CAR

[*Another girl waits with a suitcase under a bandstand. She waves and runs towards* TOPLIS. *He stops the car and hoots the horn with a certain grinning conceit.*

During the above montage we hear the voice of the prosecution counsel]

PROSECUTION [V.O.]: The defendant has indeed a history of unlawful endeavour, m'lud; most recently, July 1911, Dumfries Bench, ten days' imprisonment for non-payment of train tickets for himself, m'lud . . . and a woman companion. August of the same year, Pately Bridge Bench, one month's hard labour, theft. Of a lady's purse and four pounds.

JUDGE [V.O.]: Thank you. We have heard the touching and most convincing testimony of the victim, Miss Teresa Kelly, detailing the distress and horror of this wanton ravage. The doctor's evidence clearly indicates the girl had bruising of a serious nature – clear and categorical signs of force and violence.

11/1. INT. LINCOLN CROWN COURT QUARTER SESSIONS. DAY

[*We now see the* JUDGE *as he looks towards* TOPLIS]

JUDGE: Have you anything to say before sentence is passed?

TOPLIS [*giving it one last go*]: Yes sir. I could have a lot to say, sir, like she fell off the haystack, your honour, but she had no bruises nor black eyes when I was with her, sir, and everything was snug and handsome till her father caught us, and –

JUDGE: *Toplis, you have been found guilty.* You are wasting your time. And mine. Proceed to irritate me further at your own risk.

TOPLIS: . . . Ask her father where she got the bruises! [*stops*] . . . But sir, having been found guilty of a crime I did not commit – that at least I did not think was a crime when I was committing it – may I throw myself upon the mercy of the court, your honour. May I say that I have been an orphan, sir, since the age of four.

JUDGE: That's enough.

TOPLIS: That unhappiness and pain have been my lot since I can't remember when.

JUDGE [*bangs gavel*]: Enough.

TOPLIS: That I have searched the country in –

JUDGE [*banging the gavel*]: Enough! Enough!

TOPLIS: And I'm only fifteen, sir!

JUDGE: Francis Percy Toplis, it is the sentence of this court that you will be taken from this court to His Majesty's Prison, Lincoln, where you will stay for two years. It is the recommendation of this court that this period of imprisonment be accompanied by rigorous hard labour.

TOPLIS: Fair enough, it's all I expected, you stupid old fart.

[*He is dragged by the policemen at the base of the dock as they rush up and proceed to drag him out of court*]

I never did nothing – it was her – two years for nothing – bloody nothing! You ask her!

[*We hear sounds of violence as he is led away*]

Gerroff!

12/13/14/1. EXT. LINCOLN JAIL. DAY
LATE AUTUMN, 1914

[*Wet streets. A door opens.* TOPLIS *walks out, a spare shirt rolled up in his hand; no overcoat.*

He puts his collar up and begins to walk away, looking hard and grim-faced.

As he walks, a platoon of the Ninth (Reserve) Battalion of the Lincolnshire Regiment march past the jail, going the same way as TOPLIS.

They are raw young volunteers. Quietly and with great sentiment they sing 'It's a long way to Tipperary'. They have the idealism, romanticism and patriotism of the ignorant and battle-free.

They whistle a chorus, sing the chorus and start to whistle again]

PLATOON: It's a long way to Tipperary
It's a long way to go
It's a long way to Tipperary
To the sweetest girl I know
Goodbye Piccadilly
Farewell Leicester Square
It's a long long way to Tipperary
But my heart's right there.

[*The platoon sweeps past* TOPLIS *as he walks slowly along. He watches them as they go, sardonically, and finally spits on the floor as their singing turns to whistling. When he looks up, he sees at his side, in a post office window, posters of low-propaganda brilliance depicting the joys of Kitchener's calling*]

13/1. INT. SALVATION ARMY PENNY SIT-UP
DAY. DECEMBER 1914

[*A dreadful aircraft hangar of a place with bunks at either side of the large room, and bench after bench filling the rest of the space.*

We see TOPLIS *and the remnants of society.*

Many old tramps with unkempt beards, but a lot of younger people.

A vacancy of expression.

They are lectured to by a Salvation Army captain]

CAPTAIN: . . . And so, as this, the first Christmas of the war against Germany approaches, as we meet here today in prayer, as I look around me at those of us who are in difficult circumstances, and as our brave boys fight on foreign fields, I want you to know one thing, gentlemen. There is no Christian sin in volunteering! The blame for this war does not rest with us! Germany forced this war and will undoubtedly be punished by God. The Lord is with our armies. Our cause is right. And right must triumph over might. Yes, do not forget what the Hun has already achieved in the cause of the Devil – the shameless murder of women and children! And so I ask you, those of you who are able-bodied men, who think that perhaps life has no purpose left, who have fallen on hard times, I ask you to consider that this is the time to do your duty! Now is the time for Christians to take up the sword! [*a short benign pause*] It is but a short walk with our sergeant here, a march even, to the recruiting office in Mosspits Lane.

[*And nothing happens*]

Meanwhile, if we would all join together, before soup is served, in the singing of that most beautiful of all hymns, 'Abide with Me'.

[*We see* TOPLIS *stand up. The* CAPTAIN *smiles at him, whispers loud enough for the whole room to hear*]

CAPTAIN: Brave man!

TOPLIS: I'm going to the lavatory, what's brave about that?

[*Laughter from the others.* TOPLIS *grins at them as he walks away from them. The audience rises*]

CAPTAIN: Gentlemen.

[*Their attention returns to the* CAPTAIN *who leads them into a ragged version of 'Abide with Me'.* TOPLIS *notices the* CAPTAIN*'s coat on the bannisters. He picks up the coat and moves away downstairs, rifling through the pockets as he goes*]

AUDIENCE: Abide with me; fast falls the eventide;
The darkness deepens; Lord, with me abide!
When other helpers fail, and comforts flee,
Help of the helpless, Lord, abide with me.

Swift to its close ebbs out life's little day;
Earth's joys grow dim, its glories pass away;
Change and decay in all around I see;
O Thou who changest not, abide with me.

16/1. INT. PUBLIC HOUSE. DAY
EARLY SPRING, 1915

[*A big but near empty bar-room. There are three old men, and a table of about eight soldiers. Three or four, dressed in hospital 'blues', have been clearly wounded in action; some have crutches and sticks, one boy is in a wheelchair, another has no right arm.*

While one of them is at the bar ordering drinks, the others look with silent disdain towards the billiard table.

We see TOPLIS, *alone at the billiard table, looking as low as he will ever look until he is on the run. And deliberately playing poorly, like a rank beginner. Glances over to the old men, then the soldiers. Begins to approach the bar*]

TOPLIS: . . . Any of you lads fancy a game? Just for sport – or a bob or two if you want.

[*No answer*]

I'm a bit down on my luck at the moment . . .

FIRST SOLDIER: I know where you can get a shilling.

TOPLIS: Just for a pint then, what do you say, fellers?

[*The soldier in the wheelchair flicks at the empty sleeve of the soldier with no arm*]

WHEELCHAIR: He'll play you.

TOPLIS: Probably beat me and all.

FIRST SOLDIER: Why, what's wrong with you?

TOPLIS: Nothing.

[TOPLIS *turns to the barmaid. Young, rough, and roughly attractive. He puts a penny on the bar top*]

Half a pint of your very best, my dear.

[*She doesn't look at him at all. As she fills the glass, he looks back towards the soldiers*]

WHEELCHAIR: And then, after the billiards we can all go down the back field and have a good old game of football. Shall we, eh? I don't care what he is, Friend of Fritz or friggin' coward, what does it matter?

[TOPLIS *hears his drink being put on the bar. Turns to the bar, forcing a smile. We see his pint, with a good head, and a white feather lying on top of the froth.* TOPLIS *looks at the pint. Looks at the barmaid. She throws the farthing on the bar, folds her arms across her chest, but doesn't look at him.* TOPLIS *picks the farthing up, puts it in his pocket, and reaches finally for his pint. As he pulls it towards him he carefully takes the white feather off the top. He holds it between finger and thumb, and then quietly looks up at the ceiling for flying chickens. He then leans over the bar to look for running chickens on the floor. His eyes betray his anger as he gently enquires*]

TOPLIS: . . . You keep livestock?

[*No answer. But he barely waits for one. He flicks the feather in the air and takes his beer. He glances at the soldiers, one or two of whom leer at him, and then approaches the billiard table. He picks up his cue, briefly studies the position of the balls, and then bends down to play his shot. He batters his cue ball with venom, cracking it against the spot ball and then the red ball. The red flies into a pocket. He throws the cue on the table*]

17/1. EXT. THE FRONT LINE. COMMUNICATION TRENCH. LOOS. DAWN AND DAY

1. FROM TOPLIS'S BILLIARDS CANNON TO AN EXPLOSION. DAWN

2. INT. TOPLIS'S DUGOUT. DAWN

[*The debris from the explosion showers onto the sleeping figures of* TOPLIS, COCKNEY, GEORDIE, *etc.*]

GEORDIE: Bugger me.
COCKNEY: Who left the bloody door open?

3. EXT. DUGOUT. COMMUNICATION TRENCH

[*Some sleepers and some figures moving up to the fire trench with supplies*]

4. EXT. FIRE TRENCH. DAWN

[*Sporadic sniping. Only sentries on the firestep stand – other men are huddled everywhere wrapped in capes and blankets, being woken up quietly by a* SERGEANT *and a* CORPORAL]

5. EXT. FIRE TRENCH. DAY

[*Light barrage.*
Breakfast.
A soldier pours a sandbag full of biscuits and cheese onto a board, and divides it up, to groans of 'oh no, not biscuits again'.
Water cans for drinking.
Tea and candle to warm it]

6. EXT. FIRE TRENCH

[CAPTAIN *and* SERGEANT *inspect lined-up troops. Gun barrels, hats straight, equipment.* CORPORAL *with notebook*]

SERGEANT: Button, laddie, button. Show me the barrel. Filthy. Bloody filthy. Name and number.
SOLDIER: Cousins. 036.
SERGEANT: What's this. You can't shoot the Hun with those. Although you could infect him.

7. EXT. FIRE TRENCH

[*Rum ration* SERGEANT *and* CORPORAL *issue rum. Possible officer near by*]

8. EXT. GAS BAY

[*We see a soldier checking the direction of the wind, using a stick held in the air, with a rag on it*]

SOLDIER: It's too windy, Sarge.
[*Brings stick down*]
And it might be the wrong way.
OFFICER [*out of vision*]: I said *'Carry on, Sergeant!'*
SOLDIER [*to himself*] . . . soddin' hell . . .

9. EXT. THE TRENCHES

[*Preparing to go over the top*]

SERGEANT: . . . Fix bayonets. Step up. Gas helmets on.
[*We see the men struggling to put the grotesque masks on*]

10. EXT. MACHINE GUN BAY

[*We see the machine gunners putting their masks on. Standing by*]

11. THE TRENCHES

[*We see soldiers struggling to go over the top. Casualties immediately*]

12. INT. TOPLIS'S DUG OUT

[RAMC SERGEANT *enters, almost cheerfully.* TOPLIS*'s team brewing up, gas helmets rolled back.* TOPLIS *with cigarette*]

RAMC SERGEANT: Gas Helmets on. One Minute to Go. All right, lads?

TOPLIS: Oh, yes sir. Happy as can be.

[*He grins. A huge explosion nearby showers them. There are calls for stretcher bearers*]

18/1. EXT. TRENCHES. EXPLOSION AREA. DAY

[TOPLIS, *the* COCKNEY, *the* GEORDIE *and others race up the short distance to the front trench from communication trench in the smoke and dust.*

They see a simply horrendous sight – a high-explosive German shell has fallen right into the wider part of the trench and exploded amongst the men.

We hear groans and screams and death gasps.

We see men, many with their gas masks on, running around with gaping wounds, like chickens with their heads cut off, often deafened and shocked by the explosion, blood pouring, running into each other, into the side of the trench, bouncing and falling all over each other.

We see the STRETCHER BEARERS *knocking into each other, picking people up, trying to keep people down to get them onto stretchers.*

Gas is then released from cylinders further along the trenches, billowing across into no-man's land. But not for long.

The Germans respond with machine gun fire. Some aimed at the trench we are in, and for a time the gas is forgotten.

We see the CAPTAIN *in the midst of the action, with a wild desperation not connected with 'heroics'.*

One of the wounded men suddenly starts firing aimlessly as he screams and staggers. And men duck for cover till he falls on his rifle.

TOPLIS *and the* COCKNEY *are knocked over by one of the wounded, blood boiling from a wound in the latter's thigh as he runs madly and blindly. Another soldier hurtles past, blood pouring from his mouth.*

TOPLIS *picks himself up, and directly gets immersed underneath another man who simply topples onto him.*

TOPLIS *slides away and stands. A soldier, more blood than body, grabs him twitching feverishly, as he belches at* TOPLIS.

TOPLIS *backs into the parapet as the soldier talks to him*]

WOUNDED MAN [*almost inaudible*]: Shoot me fucking shoot me please shoot me.

[*He topples forward and* TOPLIS *swerves away from him.* TOPLIS *looks down horrified. He is grabbed away by the* COCKNEY *holding the stretcher*]

COCKNEY: He's gone, come on.

[*Then the gas, sent by the British, slowly comes back and sideways on the wind, glistening towards the trenches, just as most of the wounded are being seen to in one way or another. We also hear the feverish banging on empty gas cylinders from the trench that the gas originally came from, trying to warn our men. There are whistles and shrieks too. In the middle of trying to rescue the wounded, men are putting on gas masks or simply running away, and we see men blinded, choking and cursing, throwing down their masks and disappearing down the communication trenches. As soon as the gas starts to smear across the parapets, the* COCKNEY *grabs* TOPLIS *and pushes him*]

COCKNEY: Just get someone! Anyone!

[*They pull a man from underneath some soil and slush and debris, and throw him, groaning, onto the stretcher, before hurtling away down the communication trench as fast as they can. And we hear* TOPLIS *shouting as he goes*]

TOPLIS: That's our own gas, our own side've fuckin' gassed us . . .

[*We stay on the scene. Nobody is now left except the patently dead. As we move along the trench in the mist of the gas, we see equipment scattered everywhere – guns and masks and periscopes, hats and mugs and mess tins, blankets rolled in groundsheets, pocket Primuses, tins of tobacco, pipes, gloves, mufflers, mittens, tubes of Vaseline, stone rum bottles, food rations, a Bible, a fob watch, trampled love letters – amidst the contorted and almost dismembered dead. While, above all, we see that the trench is 'red with blood like a room papered in crimson'*]

19/1. EXT/INT. BOMBED FIELD STATION THE LINES. NIGHT

[*We see distant flashes and Verey lights.*

Inside are TOPLIS *and the other men, blankets around them, keeping them warm and keeping the light from their candles hidden, as they go through the ceremony of burning off the chatts (lice) from their uniforms.*

They sit around with candles, holding up various parts of their uniform in one hand, while, with the other, they run the candle along the seams, so that the flame cracks both the chatts and their eggs – loudly from all accounts]

TOPLIS: . . . 'Dear Mother, the Army's a bugger, sell the pig and buy me out. Your loving son John'. 'Dear John, the pig's dead, soldier on . . .'

[*Quiet chuckles. They've heard it before, but* TOPLIS *tells it well. This is the side of him that takes people with him*]

COCKNEY: . . . 'Dear Mother, I am sending you ten shillings – but not this week.'

[*Again amusement, though they will have heard that every day*]

TOPLIS: . . . Napoleon's greetings to his troops – 'Good morning, troops'.

[*More laughter*]

GEORDIE: Eh, Percy, give us your 'Circus Showman'. Away man.

[*Quite some agreement and enthusiasm.* TOPLIS *affects reluctance*]

COCKNEY: Let's have a song, lads!

GEORDIE: What shall we sing?

COCKNEY: 'Hands Across The Sea'.

EVERYONE [*fortissimo*]: 'Hands Across My Bloody Arse!'

[*Pause.* TOPLIS *snuffs his candle out, lifts the blanket off his head*]

TOPLIS: Ah sod it. They'll only be back in the morning . . .

[*Mainly to himself*]

. . . And they'll leave me soon enough when I'm cold.

[COCKNEY *pulls him to his feet*]

COCKNEY: Come on, Percy, I've never heard it. Come on.

[*As* TOPLIS *reaches centre stage he turns and takes the floor*]

TOPLIS: I thank you! First of all, welcome to the circus, ladies and gentlemen, and I trust that you ladies will forgive my French. And first of all we have the rhinoceros, the richest animal in the world. And to those of you familiar with the Classics, the derivation of its name is most interesting – 'rhino' meaning money, and 'soreass' meaning piles. There you have it, ladies and gentlemen, piles of money.

[*A few groans in good humour.* TOPLIS *frowns archly at them*]

And next, the leopard, one spot for every day of the year. 'But what about Leap Year?' you may ask. Bill, just lift his tail. I will now show you the camel. This peculiar animal eats mud, shits bricks and has a triangular arse-hole. Hence the pyramids. And here, to divert for one moment, is the Wild Man of Borneo. Poor man, he has no willy-wanger of any description. Sad but true.

GEORDIE [*on cue*]: But how does he stuff, Guvnor?

TOPLIS: He can't – that's what makes him so bloody wild. And finally, finally we have the armoured armadillo! This is an extraordinary beast. For when pursued by his foes, does he run away? NO! Does he climb trees! No! Does he turn into a commanding officer and go back to headquarters as fast as he can? No! He retreats and farts defiance at his nonplussed foes.

[TOPLIS *turns away, points at a couple of men*]

Now then, you small boys, get into the boats, the elephant's about to piss . . . thank you.

[*Whistles, groans and applause. The* RAMC SERGEANT *enters*]

RAMC SERGEANT: Thank you very much. Get a good night's sleep, lads, you're going to be busy tomorrow.

[*Indicates*]

Going up the line . . .

[*Quiet sulking disgust from the men, but no more than mumbles*]

TOPLIS: Excuse me, Sergeant, what for?

RAMC SERGEANT: We're having a party, Toplis, what do you think – General Haig, Sir John French, the Chiefs of Staff, Lloyd George, the War Cabinet and the whole Royal Family. A right bean-feast. I hope you've brought your dinner jacket, lad. You'll look right out of place without.

COCKNEY: Yeah – after the Lord Mayor's Show comes the shitcart.

RAMC SERGEANT: Very good. For someone with the cradle marks still on his arse.

COCKNEY: Ah come on, it's all a game, Sar'nt.

RAMC SERGEANT: Not half it is. And the Army's got you by the testimonials, my son, and there ain't nothing you can do about it.

[*We see* TOPLIS *looking sceptical*]

So if I were you, I'd get a good night's bo-bos. You're going to need it where you're going tomorrow.

20/1. EXT. A SHELL HOLE. NO MAN'S LAND DAY

[*In the background we can see the enemy's front-line trenches.*

Remnants of a charge of men across no man's land have managed to reach the barbed wire, but not get through it. They have been followed by other men.

We do not see this in detail for the present time. It is a quiet but bloody obscenity and near farce.

In the foreground, we see TOPLIS *and the* COCKNEY *in the shell hole, stretcher thrown down at the side of them.*

They are trying to apply make-do tourniquets to three pumping bloody holes in a soldier's body. Madly, frantically, at the same time with only two pairs of hands.

The COCKNEY *stops, looks at the man's mouth and eyes*]

COCKNEY: Forget it.

[TOPLIS *looks*]

He's gone trumpet cleaning.

TOPLIS [*flatly*]: That's gratitude for y'.

COCKNEY: . . . But what are we going to do?

[TOPLIS *looks at the* COCKNEY *jaundicedly, but the* COCKNEY *is already cautiously peeping over the edge of the shell hole*]

We can't stay here for the duration.

[*We see, perhaps from outside the shell hole, the* COCKNEY*'s head as he peeps out and surveys the scene. We see, finally,* TOPLIS*'s head, lower down as he looks out and around. Then we see the scene in more detail: the madness of the German barbed wire, men hanging dead or frenzied on it, others tryint to shove themselves and each other through small gaps in it, and going down in droves. Others struggle with and in the areas of barbed wire that the artillery have failed to break up or destroy earlier in the day. We also see the German machine gun post. We see the reserve men as they rise from their trenches and begin to advance towards* TOPLIS *and the*

COCKNEY *and the enemy line – scared, darting, zigzagging, stumbling and falling onward. We focus on one of the few officers out in the open. A Lieutenant, with a cigarette and a revolver, conducting the battle like a cricket captain at mid-off, yet not with a totally languid air. Certainly, however, offering invitation cards as he points and cajoles and applauds and pushes. We return to* TOPLIS *and the* COCKNEY, *who are looking back towards the Lieutenant. And then we see* TOPLIS *beginning to slide down into the shell hole*]

TOPLIS [*as he slides down*]: It's like watching Notts County.

COCKNEY: *It's what?*

TOPLIS: Or the Arsenal. There's bastards up there who are supposed to know what they're doin' – they've been trained for years for all this – we're just the crowd. But any fool in the crowd can see – the artillery never broke enough of the wire, so what idiot gave the order to go over the top?

[COCKNEY *seeing something as he peeps out*]

COCKNEY: Perce –

TOPLIS: I shouldn't be here –

COCKNEY: No –

TOPLIS: *And I'm not going to die here.*

COCKNEY: Look at this – you won't believe this.

[*We see the shambles of the first group of soldiers retreating from the enemy trenches, as the reserve troops begin to reach and attack the enemy trenches. All, inevitably, coming under heavy fire from the enemy trenches further back. The reserve attack mix with the first of the retreating men, in a collective mêlée of more madness. Amidst the shouting and screaming and jostling, the gun fire and shelling continues. A soldier, blood pumping from a shoulder wound, spins into the shell hole beside them, in panic and shock. Then shouts of 'Get back, get back', that well-known Beatles' song, are heard from the soldiers between them and the enemy lines, as everyone begins to retreat*]

SOLDIER [*in panic*]: I'm sorry, Bill.

COCKNEY: Eh?

SOLDIER: D'you hear me, Billy?

[TOPLIS *is ready to scramble, ignoring the soldier in panic*]

TOPLIS: Get in front of the retreat, we'll be covered, come on!

SOLDIER [*in panic*]: Honest, Bill.

COCKNEY: What about him?

TOPLIS: Jesus Christ!

SOLDIER [*in panic*]: Look at me, Bill, look at me. Billy?

[*The* COCKNEY *floors him with a haymaker to the chin. As the retreat nears them, we see* TOPLIS *and the* COCKNEY *pulling the* SOLDIER *in panic onto the stretcher, talking quickly as they hurl him on*]

TOPLIS: Who's turn is it at the back, Jim?

COCKNEY: You know who's turn it is – come on!

[*It is* TOPLIS*'s turn. We see the pair of them gallop out of the shell hole towards their own parapets. The retreat protects them to a degree. They approach the Lieutenant, now a solitary figure, twenty yards from his own line, waving his gun wildly as the retreat passes him by. When* TOPLIS *and the* COCKNEY *are less than five yards from him, a sniper's bullet hits him in the neck and he is instantly and obviously, from* TOPLIS*'s and the* COCKNEY*'s point of view, very dead before he hits the floor, face up in front of them. They race straight past him, and, reaching the trenches, hurl themselves in*]

21/1. EXT. TRENCHES. DAY

[*The* SOLDIER *in panic sits up. He is bounced off the stretcher*]

SOLDIER [*in panic*]: What are you doing here, Billy? You're dead, Bill.

[*He gallops off down the trenches as the* COCKNEY *makes a grab at him*]

TOPLIS: Unlucky, Bill.

[*They begin to laugh, but are stopped immediately by a* CAPTAIN *who runs shouting at them, with a wildness of a man suddenly past his limit*]

CAPTAIN: You two – you and your friend – here!

[*They don't have to go anywhere. He is already with them, grabbing*]

Come over the lid with me. Lieutenant Mellor's out there wounded!

TOPLIS: No he's not. He's dead, he's got two great big holes in him y' could put y' fist through.

CAPTAIN: *I'm ordering you.*

TOPLIS: Fuck off.

CAPTAIN [*screaming*]: Lieutenant Mellor's out there injured and under fire.

TOPLIS: No, he's not – he's dead. We look after the wounded – you can have the medals.

CAPTAIN: *He's my best friend.*

TOPLIS: He was.

[CAPTAIN *draws his pistol.* COCKNEY *comes between them*]

COCKNEY: Sir, there'll be men here who'll die if we don't get them back.

SOLDIER [*in panic, far off*]: Billy, I'm comin', Bill.

CAPTAIN: I order you to get out there now, and if you don't I'll shoot you dead *here and now*!

COCKNEY: Come on. Come on.

[*As* TOPLIS and the CAPTAIN *stare at each other with mutual wild loathing, the* COCKNEY *makes* TOPLIS*'s decision for him and calls* TOPLIS *to the parapets. The* CAPTAIN *follows. They reach the top of the parapet, ready to go.* TOPLIS *and the* COCKNEY *half stand ready to sprint. The* CAPTAIN, *between them, stands. He is shot dead. He slides down the parapet.* TOPLIS *and the* COCKNEY *dive back into the trenches. They slump against the side and the* CAPTAIN, *still in the trench*]

TOPLIS [*flatly*]: . . . Heroes . . .

[*The* SOLDIER *in panic runs past*]

SOLDIER [*in panic*]: Goodbye, Bill, goodbye . . .

22/1. EXT. TRENCHES NEAR A DUG OUT. DUSK

[*A couple of weeks later.*

Several of the stretcher bearers we have already established are watching an RAMC *going away*]

SERGEANT: Right lad.

RAMC: Right Sarg.

[*We see the* SERGEANT *disappearing. The* GEORDIE *follows, looks around a corner after him*]

GEORDIE: He's gone.

[*We see a hand come out of the shadows of the dugout, holding a stolen rum bottle. We see that the hand belongs to none other than* PERCY TOPLIS. *He comes out of the shadows, holding his own bottle. Drinks from it and passes it on. The look-out returns*]

Jesus . . . How do you do it, Perce?

TOPLIS [*lightly*]: Like most of us – right handed with the light out.

[*They grin and begin to drink, now no longer noticing that they are sitting in mud and slime and debris.* TOPLIS, *sitting next to the* COCKNEY, *notices that he is inspecting an ornate and pretty tin box, almost on purpose*]

TOPLIS: Hey buggerlugs, that's mine.

COCKNEY: Huh, it's not, it's mine now.

TOPLIS: I found it first.

COCKNEY: It was covered in mud and you gave it to me.

TOPLIS: Yeah. Only to clean up and polish. Come on. Let's play fair – we won't argue – we'll share it – yours and mine – we'll make it ours. All right, brovver?

COCKNEY: Okay – it's ours. But I'll keep it for us.

[*He laughs*]

TOPLIS: Fair enough, if that's the way y'want it, it's fine by me.

[*The* COCKNEY *is about to have a bottle passed to him.* TOPLIS *leans across him and takes the bottle himself. He drinks from it long and hard as the* COCKNEY *looks at him, just slightly unsure*]

TOPLIS: Just like that box, Jimmy – we're sharing this rum, but I'm drinking it.

[*The others laugh*]

GEORDIE: You sod.

[TOPLIS *goes to pass it along, away from the* COCKNEY, *then gives it back to him. As the* COCKNEY *drinks,* TOPLIS *still looks at the box. He does have a certain regret now, that he gave it away*]

TOPLIS: Too nice for you, that box. And you've got nothin' to put in it.

COCKNEY: What about all me love letters. Hey, hey?

[*Enjoying his moment*]

And then there's my . . . personal papers . . . not forgetting my little leave pass here.

[*The* COCKNEY *takes the papers out of his tunic pocket and takes great delight in dropping them into the box as the others groan and boo*]

TOPLIS [*taking the bottle*]: You mention that once more . . .

COCKNEY: Heh-heh-heh-heh-heh . . . Won't be long now. No more ham shanks for me. There we'll be, Pauline and me, givin' it the old one two!

[*They look up and see that the* RAMC SERGEANT *has quietly returned – no chance of hiding the bottles. Caught rum-handed. The* SERGEANT *approaches and stands in front of* TOPLIS. TOPLIS *looks up and gives him his Lincoln Crown Court look of innocence. The* SERGEANT *responds warmly. Happily even*]

RAMC SERGEANT: I've been watching you, laddie. The both of you.

[*Nods towards the* COCKNEY]

And you know what – you two, but especially you, Toplis, you get away with murder . . . And the rest of the men let you. You know why that is?

TOPLIS: . . . No Sar'nt.

RAMC SERGEANT: They think you're . . . a laugh, Toplis. They think you're lucky. Men put a lot of store in that. They want to be near someone what's lucky. They think it rubs off . . .

[*He lets it sink in, as he bends down and takes the stone rum bottle away from* TOPLIS]

. . . But you've just run out of luck, my son.

[*As they leave*]

I'm glad you volunteered, saved me a lot of heartache, that has . . .

23/1. EXT. QUARRY AND SITE HUT. NIGHT

[*Hurricane lamps shining through the windows as the* SERGEANT *and* TOPLIS *walk down towards it, in silence.*

The SERGEANT *still carries the rum bottle.*

There is a guard on the door of the site hut.

When the SERGEANT *finally speaks, it is low key and gentle.*]

RAMC SERGEANT: You won't have too much to do tonight. Though someone might faint . . . you might faint.

TOPLIS: Sar'nt?

RAMC SERGEANT: We've been asked to send someone to sit up all night with . . . a sick man. He's not expected to live very long.

[*The* GUARD *salutes the* SERGEANT. *They stand in front of the door. The* SERGEANT *gives* TOPLIS *the rum bottle. The* SERGEANT *walks away*]

24/1. INT. QUARRY. HUT. NIGHT/DAWN

[TOPLIS *looks through the flap into the hut.*

Inside we see two other guards sitting either side of a table, while at the side of the table we see a young, fresh-faced, totally terrified soldier, dressed as a private.

In front of him is a large mug of rum.
In total on the table there are three glasses and one bottle.
One of the guards is a Corporal. He is drinking too.
The younger of the guards is not drinking.
Both men sit there, ashen-faced and barely able to look at the young man at the head of the table.
TOPLIS *takes in the scene.*
He goes in and closes the door.
TOPLIS *sits.*
The young man looks at him, big-eyed.
TOPLIS *pours himself a drink.*
Silence – for what seems like forever]

TOPLIS: I hate these bars with no pianos.

[TOPLIS *winces at his faux pas and the deathly reaction. Half raises his glass in 'cheers'. Stops himself. But not before the young man has seen him*]

YOUNG MAN [*raising his glass*]: Good health! A long life and a merry one.

[*The* YOUNG MAN *throws the drink down himself*]

Oh yes, I'll drink to that.

[*The* YOUNG MAN *laughs wildly. Stops.* FIRST GUARD, *an older man, a Corporal in his thirties*]

FIRST GUARD: Steady on, chum.

YOUNG MAN: Why? Huh? Why? I see no reason to 'steady on'. 'Chum'. Do you? Do either of you? . . . What about you – Royal Army Medical Corp? Or as we used to know you 'Rob All My Comrades'. You've heard that, haven't you? 'Rob All My Comrades'. The sleeping and the dead.

TOPLIS: Yes, I've heard it. There's others . . . 'Run Away, Mother's Coming' . . . 'Rats after Mouldy Cheese'.

FIRST GUARD [*sharply*]: Body snatchers.

[TOPLIS *nods in acknowledgement*]

YOUNG MAN: We're about the same size – are you going to rob all my clothes when this is over? Mmmmmm?

TOPLIS [*evenly*]: No. I'm only interested in officers . . . and their uniforms.

[*They stare at each other.* TOPLIS *smiles at him. The* YOUNG MAN *crumbles. Speaks genuinely when he finally finds the words*]

YOUNG MAN: I'm sorry. I'm so sorry. I'm very sorry.

[*He stands up*]

FIRST GUARD: Sit down.
YOUNG MAN: Why?
FIRST GUARD: 'Cos I can hardly stand up meself. *Now sit down.*
[*The* YOUNG MAN *sits down*]
SECOND GUARD: Can't I have a drink, Corp?
FIRST GUARD: *No.*
YOUNG MAN: What time is it?
FIRST GUARD: We don't know.
YOUNG MAN: What's your name?
TOPLIS: Percy.
YOUNG MAN: I bet you're even younger than me, aren't you?
[*No answer*]
I'm twenty, Percy. How old are you?
TOPLIS: Younger than you.
YOUNG MAN: Do you want to know something? It's a secret.
[*No answer*]
I said – do you want to know something, Percy?
TOPLIS: 'It's a secret'. You said that as well.
YOUNG MAN: But do you?
TOPLIS [*shrugs*]: Go on.
YOUNG MAN [*leaning forward*]: You see, I am an officer . . . I *was* an officer. I funked it. Old boy. I shat it. As they say . . . Do you want to . . .
[*Stops*]
. . . I don't suppose you'd want to know why, would you?
TOPLIS: Tell me if you want. I don't really mind.
YOUNG MAN: We were on a ridge just to the south of here . . . asking for it . . . and we got it . . . three days and nights of bombardment . . . all the heavy stuff, it was great fun, the dawn . . .
[*Laughs*]
. . . the dawn of the fourth day, told to advance . . . the stuff still coming . . . I was the only officer left, all the others were dead, stood there with what was left of the platoon, the men all waiting for me. And I shat it. Right there in front of all the men. Dropped my pistol and ran away. Screaming my silly head off.
FIRST GUARD [*suddenly*]: Are you Cruikshank?
[*The* YOUNG MAN *nods*]
I've heard about you.
[*Carries on drinking.* TOPLIS *for a second contemplates lacerating him*]

YOUNG MAN [*after drinking some more*]: They didn't know whether to court martial me for . . . 'shamefully casting away my arms in the presence of the enemy' or 'behaving in a cowardly manner'. They chose the latter. I think it was easier to spell . . . Officers, however, don't behave like cowards, did you know that? It's not allowed. And if they do . . . nobody must know. So . . . so before my court martial I was . . .

[*This hurts*]

. . . I lost my commission.

[*Tries to laugh, fails*]

Off went my pips . . . I was court martialled as a private.

[*Finally leans back*]

Now that's a secret. Very few people know that. And soon there'll be one less to tell the tale. *I want to stand up.*

FIRST GUARD [*in his cups*]: Oh Jesus . . . go on if you have to. Cover the door, Pottsy.

[*The* SECOND GUARD *gets sluggishly to his feet, moves to the door. The* YOUNG MAN *walks up and down, up and down at the far end of the room. The* SECOND GUARD, *no more than nineteen, leans against the door.* TOPLIS *lights a cigarette*]

YOUNG MAN: They promised not to tell my mother. They were very nice about it. It was like being back at school . . . What time is it?

FIRST GUARD: *We don't know.*

YOUNG MAN: I can't get drunk. I can't.

[*Reaches for drink*]

I have tried.

FIRST GUARD: Keep trying.

[*We fade as the* YOUNG MAN *walks and drinks. We return as the light of dawn looks for means of entry. The* FIRST GUARD *has his head down on his arms, just about awake. The* SECOND GUARD *stares out as he sits on the floor, leaning against the door, smoking.* TOPLIS *is low in his seat, legs out, shirt undone, drunk but not glazed or gone. The* YOUNG MAN *is still walking. Still drinking, still sober, still talking*]

YOUNG MAN: Seahouses in the summer, on the train with mother and father and Julia and Liddy and . . . baby Stephen. Father's blasted pipe tobacco.

[*Laughs*]

My God, all the way from York. Have you been to York, Percy?

TOPLIS: Yes. I did some . . . business there once.

YOUNG MAN: When we were at Seahouses, we rode white horses on the beach beneath the castle . . . it was never very warm, there was often an East wind off the sea . . . off the North Sea. An East wind off the North Sea, Percy.

TOPLIS: Yes.

YOUNG MAN: Very few people know how beautiful Northumberland is, you know, I'm a virgin, I've never been with a woman, I'm twenty-one next . . . I'm twenty, and I've . . . and I never will now, will I? You'd like Seahouses, Percy. You must go there. They'll remember me there. What time is it, please what time is it?

FIRST GUARD: We haven't got the time.

[*Looks up*]

You can have a drink now, Pottsy.

[*Puts his head down again*]

SECOND GUARD: Thanks, Corp.

[*The* SECOND GUARD *stands up to get the drink.* TOPLIS *is looking out of the window. We see some officers sauntering towards the site. In the distance are a dozen soldiers approaching on a troop carrier led by a Sergeant-Major. They assemble. It is not the best marching that the British Army has ever accomplished*]

YOUNG MAN: What's happening?

TOPLIS: Nothing.

YOUNG MAN: There should be. I mean . . . it's very nearly dawn. Isn't it?

[*No answer*]

I used to like the dawn. When I was at home, I always used to – if this was winter, I'd live longer –

[*Screams*]

I don't want to go, I don't want to go!

[*The* YOUNG MAN *slumps huddled in a corner, shaking and crying*]

I never ran away before. Never. Never . . . not once.

[*There is a knock on the door. The* YOUNG MAN *jumps. The* GUARD *on the door looks through the flap and nods towards the* CORPORAL. *A Captain waits outside*]

FIRST GUARD: I'm sorry. Come on.

YOUNG MAN: No. No.

FIRST GUARD: Look, you've got to go now.

YOUNG MAN: No, I'm not going. It's not fair. *I couldn't help it!*

[*We see the two* GUARDS *begin to approach the* YOUNG MAN. *We see* TOPLIS *turn away and stare through the window*]

25/1. EXT. QUARRY FIRING SQUAD. DAY

[*The firing squad arrive in the troop carrier and line up*]

SERGEANT MAJOR: Fall in single file. Come on. Straighten up.
[*Ten men are lined up waiting. Some are patently, almost implausibly, drunk, already horrified at the prospect.* A SERGEANT MAJOR *stands at the side of the men, watching them. Particularly one man. Who may be short and tubby, but is clearly unable to keep a proper balance, and is about to faint or throw up, or both*]
Squad turn.
[*Another man begins to shake. He is joined by another. The* SERGEANT MAJOR *walks down the line, whispering murderously*]
Any man – any man – and I know you're all pissed as farts – but any man makes a fool of himself makes a fool of me. And woe betide that man . . . you, stop shaking now. Now! . . . that bastard ran away, he left men like yourselves to fend for themselves, he was a coward and he couldn't cope, but you're going to cope, because if you don't . . . [*We see a small knot of officers. The* RAMC SERGEANT *and the* COCKNEY *are by the site hut. Behind the chair and the post are two Privates. And out of the door of the hut, led struggling and manic, comes the* YOUNG MAN. *He is forced across to the chair, where still struggling and crying, he is bound by his ankles and his wrists and then blindfolded. While* TOPLIS *watches with eyes like we saw in Mansfield in 1908, the* MEDICAL OFFICER *pins a white handkerchief in the shape of a triangle over the* YOUNG MAN*'s heart.* TOPLIS *approaches and stands by the* COCKNEY. *They look, all expression drained. We see the soldiers in line, well gone by now. The order to raise arms is given. We see several shaky rifles, barely a still hand in sight. The* YOUNG MAN *has tears leaking through the blindfold, as he still attempts to free himself from the ropes attached to the chair. The officer gives the signal*]
MAJOR: Sergeant Major.
SERGEANT MAJOR: Squad. With one round load. Present arms.
YOUNG MAN: *Mother!*
SERGEANT MAJOR: Fire.
[*Ten rifles go off, hardly together and all over the place. The sign on the hut much to the right of the* YOUNG MAN *in the chair is hit by a bullet.*
Unload. Stand still.
[*They see that their intended victim is still alive. Still blindfolded.*

And attempting to run away while still attached to the chair and the snapped-off post. Blood is running freely from a chest wound, but he staggers on instinctively towards the men who shot him. The officer in charge steps forward, takes a pistol out of his holster and points it, shakily, at the YOUNG MAN*'s temple as he struggles on. We see three men in the firing line faint clear away as we hear the sound of the bullet. One soldier is sick all down his tunic as he tries to stand to attention*]

Straighten up. Get hold of yourselves now. Get hold of yourselves.

[*The* MEDICAL OFFICER *uses a stethoscope to check the obvious, quickly, before walking away. The* CHAPLAIN *mumbles above the body in an aloof and disdainful manner. The* RAMC SERGEANT *motions to* TOPLIS *and the* COCKNEY *to use their stretcher. They approach the body and the* CHAPLAIN *as he stoops over the body and unfastens a silver cross and chain from around the* YOUNG MAN*'s neck*]

CHAPLAIN [*to* TOPLIS]: See that goes with Private Cruikshank's personal effects.

[*The* CHAPLAIN *drops the cross and chain into* TOPLIS*'s hand. We see* TOPLIS *cover* CRUIKSHANK*'s body as everyone else walks away*]

SERGEANT MAJOR [O.O.V]: You two pick that man up. At the short trail. By the front. Quick march. Left Right. Left Right . . .

26/1. INT. LARGE HUT. LIKE A QUARTERMASTER'S STORE. THE SAME MORNING

[*Full of dead men's army clothes and personal possessions in rows and boxes, listed alphabetically.*

The soldier 'in charge' sits at a desk with his feet up, reading 'John Bull'.

We see TOPLIS *and the* COCKNEY *staring vacantly at the boxes and boxes and boxes.*

Behind them, the lines of clothing]

TOPLIS: *What do you* – ! . . . I mean!
COCKNEY: . . . What?
TOPLIS: Nothing.

[*Silence.* TOPLIS *shakes his head. They stand there. The* COCKNEY *gets out a cigarette; his hands are shaking.* TOPLIS *flicks through some of the officers' clothing*]

. . . I've done some things, Jimmy, I've pulled some stunts that, if I was bothered, I'd be ashamed of . . . I'll do some more, no doubt. I hope so . . . But *that*! That was . . .!

COCKNEY: . . . It's . . .

[COCKNEY *waves his hands helplessly*]

TOPLIS: A joke.

COCKNEY: A game. And you can't change anything. Short and curlies. Army rules. Testimonials . . . Mine are shrinking fast.

TOPLIS: Oh no. Oh fucking no!

[*He swings at the row of uniforms*]

Come on, Jimmy.

COCKNEY: What hopes.

TOPLIS [*with absolute passion*]: Listen, that's what they want – that's what they want you to want . . . that's what they want you to do – they want you to give in – they want you to be 'yes sir, no sir' – to stand and obey and be subwhatsits. And if that happens, y'may as well throw y'self in front of the nearest whizzbang. 'Cos that's what they want an' all . . . is that what you want – to find your pieces among four platoons?

[*The* COCKNEY *tries to shrug it off. As he talks, we should be aware that* TOPLIS *becomes more and more interested in the uniforms*]

COCKNEY: . . . Maybe it'll get better . . . yeah. Y'never know – a push, some advance, get them on the run. A breakthrough.

[*The* COCKNEY *sees* TOPLIS *sneering at his whimsy and stops. The* SOLDIER IN CHARGE *shouts across*]

SOLDIER IN CHARGE: . . . C.

TOPLIS [*looking around*]: See what?

SOLDIER IN CHARGE: That's U.

COCKNEY: Who's you?

SOLDIER IN CHARGE: You want 'C'. You're looking under 'U'.

[*He smiles. It is his only pleasure in life*]

TOPLIS: O.

[*They walk further down towards 'C'*]

COCKNEY: . . . You make it sound so easy, Perce. But what can we *do* – what can any of us do? You do a lot, and you can't do anything.

TOPLIS: *Can't I?*

27/1. INT. A SMALL NONDESCRIPT ROOM

[*We see* TOPLIS *and the* COCKNEY *in a small nondescript room.*
Both are dressing as officers.
TOPLIS *goes to look out of the window and returns to the* COCKNEY]

COCKNEY: These boots are tight.

TOPLIS: Yeah well you can take them off when you get down the brothel.

COCKNEY: An *officers'* brothel?

TOPLIS: Oh yes.

COCKNEY: Oh no.
[*Stops getting dressed*]
Not me. It's all right for you, but I'll be rumbled. Bound to. If I open my north and south, I'll be finished, Perce.

TOPLIS: I shall be with you, old boy. I shall take our fellow officers aside and tell them about your meteoric rise through the ranks, your heroic actions, the storming of Hill 70 . . .

COCKNEY: How do you do it all, Perce? Eh? Come on . . . the posh voice and the long words and that?

TOPLIS: Education, my boy. A very good finishing school . . . Lincoln Jail with a toff doing three years for fraud. A gentleman's crime. Now are you going to be a good boy and a gentleman too?
[*We see the uncertain* COCKNEY]

28.29/1. EXT. NEAR THE DRIVEWAY TO THE BROTHEL. NIGHT

[TOPLIS *and* COCKNEY *in officers' uniform.*
Two soldiers giving both men first-class salutes.
The COCKNEY *hardly knows where to put himself in reply, as* TOPLIS *sweeps past*]

TOPLIS: There you are, you see – easy.
[TOPLIS *glances at the* COCKNEY*'s decoration*]
By the way, I want the ribbon back afterwards.

COCKNEY: Er yeah . . . er why am I the Captain, Perce?

TOPLIS: Because the Second Lieutenant's uniform has a certain sentimental meaning to me, old boy . . .

[*Grins at him*]

Try not to slouch, Goddard.

[*We see and hear the brothel in the distance.* TOPLIS *is strutting towards it. There are* MILITARY POLICE *at the entrance*]

COCKNEY: I can't. I just can't. I'm going.

TOPLIS: Jimmy.

COCKNEY: Nah, honest mate, I'd love to, but I can't. Give them one for me . . .

TOPLIS: I'm already giving them one for someone else. And you'll be all right.

COCKNEY: Nah, I'm going on leave next week, why risk it now? And I'd never wangle it anyway, Perce. It's not me, I can't do the rabbit like you.

[*The* COCKNEY *takes hold of* TOPLIS *by the shoulders and looks towards the brothel*]

Shit! . . . Listen, have a *bon* time. Sir!

[*He salutes, smiles and turns to go – not even down the drive, but through the trees.* TOPLIS *watches him for a second or two, then turns towards the mansion. Straightens up, finds his airs, and approaches. A relatively attractive* LADY OF THE AFTERNOON *is coming out of the doorway with a distinctly unattractive overweight drunken officer. She smiles, he turns away. She stops smiling as he stumbles off. We perhaps stay with her briefly as she starts smiling again. We see* TOPLIS *as he goes past the weaving overweight drunken officer.* TOPLIS *sweeps past the two* MILITARY POLICEMEN *who salute respectfully. He goes towards the* LADY OF THE AFTERNOON]

AFTERNOON LADY: *Bonjour*, Johnny. I call you Johnny, yes?

[*She takes* TOPLIS*'s arm*]

TOPLIS: No. Call me Cruikshank. Lieutenant Cruikshank.

[*He smiles and allows her to link his arm as he struts towards the doorway, the noise and revelry. Perhaps another lady of the afternoon is at the doorway with another sluggish slug of an officer, and we just catch the briefest glance of envy from her*]

30/1. EXT. THE FRONT LINE. TRENCHES. DAY

[*The corner of the communication trench and front line trench. Seen from a position at the very back of the communication trench.*

We hear the whizz-bangs, screams, gun fire, grunts, howls and obscenities, war cries, over the tops, falling down dead, blood-letting of the front line, as men and incidents scatter past the junction of the communication and front line trenches.

TOPLIS *comes into view at the top of the communication trench, carrying a body. A body that we never identify clearly, but can only assume about later.*

TOPLIS *is screaming, running wildly with the stretcher for as long as we can hold on him. Running, running, running, back towards the dressing station with all the urgency he possesses. Still screaming as he runs, he goes past his* SERGEANT *and* GEORDIE *as they carry their stretcher towards the front line trench*]

SERGEANT: Geordie.

[*They both drop their stretchers when they see who is on the back of* TOPLIS*'s stretcher. Both men scatter after* TOPLIS. *The* SERGEANT *is the fastest. He reaches the back of the stretcher, scoops it up, almost falling in the process.* TOPLIS *runs and falls down with* COCKNEY *on top of him.* TOPLIS *is beside himself, as we have never seen him before. And will never see again*]

31/1. EXT. DUGOUT. THE TRENCHES. NIGHT

[TOPLIS *seems to be genuinely shocked as he sits in the dugout. He finally looks around – no-one in sight. He looks towards the* COCKNEY*'s kit bag. Just looks at it, then lifts it up, and holds it, almost as in an embrace.*

He opens it and looks at the Captain's uniform. Then lifts out the ornate and pretty tin, holds it closed for a second and then opens it.

There are indeed a few love letters in there. He takes out the COCKNEY*'s leave papers, glances at them and puts them back into the tin before putting the tin into his tunic pocket*]

32/1. EXT. THE WEBSTER'S HOUSE. A WEEK LATER LATE AUTUMN, 1915. BY THE BLACKWELL PIT

[*See* PERCY TOPLIS *in a Captain's dress uniform. With the distinguished conduct ribbon discreetly above the left pocket*]

BOY: Left right left right . . .

[*Some children are carrying his bag.* ANNIE WEBSTER *sees* TOPLIS *and runs from the kitchen down the path*]

ANNIE: Frank!

[TOPLIS *moves towards* ANNIE WEBSTER]

BOY: Halt.

[TOPLIS *embraces* ANNIE. FRANK *appears in the doorway*]

FRANK: Come here, y'little bugger, I want a word with you!

33/1. INT. BLACKWELL MINERS' CLUB. THAT NIGHT

[*Perhaps out of disbelief or any excuse for a celebration, but the room is packed – and waiting. Among the many middle-aged men, we see* JOHN THOMAS TODD *and* JOHNSON *at the head of the head table, champagne ready, suits on, brows still glistening with sweat. After all these years.*

And TOPLIS *arrives through the doorway, pleased to be home and honoured and humble – and 'all this for me?'.*

UNCLE FRANK, *in a new suit, comes in close behind him, quite stunned by the applause that spontaneously greets* TOPLIS *upon his arrival.*

Men stand and cheer TOPLIS *to the top table, watching him as he limps through the room.*

TOPLIS *reaches the table occupied by* TODD, JOHNSON, *two veterans of the Boer War, and what passes for civic dignitaries in Blackwell.*

TODD *grips his hand like a long-lost son;* JOHNSON *too.* JOHNSON *holds up* TOPLIS*'s hand in victory, and to applause.*

TOPLIS *makes a gesture of overwhelmed modesty, then insists that* UNCLE FRANK *be accommodated at the top table too.*

FRANK *is placed at the table.* TODD *bangs on the table for order*]

TODD: Gentlemen, *gentlemen.* Thank you. I'm not in the habit of making formal speeches, and I'll keep this brief –

TOPLIS [*languidly*]: Thank God for that.

[*A lot of laughter*]

TODD: Yes. Ever the one for a joke, as I remember – a bit of a lad at times. But as I'm sure you all know by now, we have amongst us, in our small community, our little pit village, we have amongst us a returning hero!

[*Murmurs of assent*]

A boy, if I may say, still hardly more than a mere slip of a lad, who in the past months has obviously made a man of himself, and in doing so, has done us proud.

[*More agreement*]

As I promised, I'll keep this brief –

[*Looks towards* TOPLIS *and smiles*]

– and so, gentlemen, may I give you the toast –

[*They all stand and raise their glasses*]

God Save the King!

[*They all drink.* TODD *gets slightly carried away*]

. . . England and St George and the defeat of the Hun!

[*They drink again, then sit down.* TOPLIS *affects the most touching reluctance to speak – until forced by all around him*]

TOPLIS: Gentlemen. Thank you. I will gladly keep this brief. And I am sure you will forgive this . . . mere slip of a lad's nervousness at being celebrated in such manner for what was, if the truth be told, hardly anything at all.

[*He smiles modestly at them*]

All I would like to say is that having seen what I have seen on the battlefields of France, I wish I had the words to make you believe that . . . what I have seen is what is really happening over there.

[*He sits down to congratulations and applause. And then, with his head down, as they stand and applaud, he finishes his speech*]

– but there again, none of you fatheads would listen.

34/1. INT. BLACKWELL MINERS' CLUB. NIGHT

[*The end of the night.*

But TOPLIS, *at the piano, is still solidly surrounded by 'the fat-headed crowd' of admirers and gawpers, pints in hand, finishing a patriotic song*]

MEN: Keep the home fires burning
While your hearts are yearning
Though your lads are far away
They dream of home.
There's a silver lining
Through the dark cloud shining
Turn the dark cloud inside out
Till the boys come home.

[*Sentimental applause as* TODD *leans at him*]

TODD: What I asked you before, if you remember, Percy. It would be much appreciated.

TOPLIS: It'd be a pleasure. Todd.

[TODD *stands and bangs for attention.* TOPLIS *plays rallying chords*]

TODD: Thank you, thank you. I should just like to say that Captain Toplis has very generously agreed to honour our Voluntary Training Corps by taking the drill next Saturday afternoon.

JOHNSON: And on behalf of pit-management I'd like to present you with this token of our esteem.

[JOHNSON *and* TODD *leer at* TOPLIS *as* JOHNSON *hands him a bottle of whisky, which* PERCY *opens and swigs. Cheers*]

See, lad, we look after our own here.

35/1. INT. DRAWING ROOM. CRUIKSHANK HOUSE YORK. DAY

[*The same week. Mid-afternoon.*

A well-dressed middle-aged woman is sitting at a desk writing a letter. The MAID *comes in*]

MAID: Beg pardon, ma'am. There's a gentleman here wishing to know if you are at home.

MRS CRUIKSHANK: Yes?

[TOPLIS, *uninvited, appears in the doorway, resplendent in his dress uniform. He smiles reassuringly at* MRS CRUIKSHANK. *She whispers plaintively and rises.*

Yes?

TOPLIS: I hope you don't mind me arriving unannounced, Mrs Cruikshank. It's with regard to your son, Anthony.

MRS CRUIKSHANK: You . . . you were a friend?

TOPLIS: We were very close to each other.

MRS CRUIKSHANK: Oh. Oh dear.

[MRS CRUIKSHANK *tries for an embrace that is formal, but fails*]

Oh thank you. Thank you.

36/1. INT. DRAWING ROOM. CRUIKSHANK HOUSE DAY

[TOPLIS *is sitting on the couch.*
Afternoon tea has been served.
MRS CRUIKSHANK *has recovered most of her poise and is sitting on a chair, brought nearer to* TOPLIS, *leaning forward*]

MRS CRUIKSHANK: And you came all the way to York to see me?
TOPLIS: I promised, you see. I said I would, if . . .
[*Looks at her*]
. . . Do you know how he met . . . his . . .?
MRS CRUIKSHANK: Killed on active service.
[*Bitterly, despite herself*]
A telegram, then a duplicated letter, with . . . Anthony's name and . . . particulars filling in the gaps.
TOPLIS [*with a little surprise*]: Nothing more?
MRS CRUIKSHANK: A letter from his commanding officer, but . . . abrupt, in a way. My sister, she lost her eldest boy at Ypres, and . . . the response from his commanding officer, his friends' letters, were . . . effusive and loving, but Anthony . . .
[*She fights back the tears*]
Nothing like that. Nothing . . . It's strange, Maurice, but in Anthony's letters . . . he never mentioned you . . .
TOPLIS: Well it was near the end, Mrs Cruikshank, that we really got to know each other well. We talked of the times we had as lads. Very similar actually. He spoke of the holidays in Seahouses with particular affection. Of yourself and his sisters . . . the family . . . riding horses on the beach . . .
MRS CRUIKSHANK: . . . How did he die, Maurice?
TOPLIS: With a very special kind of bravery, Mrs Cruikshank. Outnumbered, blinded and stumbling, he still kept running towards the guns. I was very near to him when it happened . . . Two of us carried him back. But he was already . . .
MRS CRUIKSHANK: Did he . . . Did Anthony say anything before he died?
TOPLIS: Yes, Mrs Cruikshank. He said one word. Very clearly. He said, 'Mother'.
[*We fade as Mrs Cruikshank weeps long and silently. We come back*

to the scene. We see that MRS CRUIKSHANK *has again regained most of her composure. Afternoon tea has been removed. The scene must convey the fact that* TOPLIS *has made her far happier than she has ever been since her son's death.* MRS CRUIKSHANK *moves from the mantelpiece and stands facing* TOPLIS]

MRS CRUIKSHANK: . . . I cannot begin to tell you what your visit has meant to me. If you would only stay a little longer, my husband would be delighted to –

TOPLIS: I should dearly love to. Unfortunately . . .

MRS CRUIKSHANK: You have a train to catch?

TOPLIS: I *did* have a train to catch. However, I do suspect I shall have to find other ways of returning to London.

MRS CRUIKSHANK: Oh, why is that?

TOPLIS: I've had some bad luck, I'm afraid. I stayed in a hotel last night and . . . well, my wallet and cheque book were taken by some thief in the night.

[*Stands up*]

But I don't want to burden you with my troubles, I'm sure I can . . .

MRS CRUIKSHANK: My dear boy. Why didn't you say?

[*She hurries to her purse*]

TOPLIS: No, no please. I insist.

MRS CRUIKSHANK: And so do I. Now then, tell me, how much will you need? And I will not take 'no' for an answer.

TOPLIS: I promise you, as soon as I get back to the battalion –

MRS CRUIKSHANK [*waving him away*]: Yes, yes. Will two guineas be enough?

TOPLIS: It would normally be highly generous of you, Mrs Cruikshank, however there is a small matter of the hotel bill . . .

[*He smiles at her*]

. . . I thought I would be safe in a good hotel but . . .

[MRS CRUIKSHANK *takes a five-pound note out of her purse and offers it to* TOPLIS]

Now, I promise you the minute I get back to the regiment, Mrs Cruikshank, the very minute . . .

[*He takes the money*]

MRS CRUIKSHANK: Do you know where they will be sending you next?

TOPLIS: No ma'am. But I for one intend to keep my head down. One way or another. After all that has happened to . . .

MRS CRUIKSHANK: Some would call that cowardice, I suppose, but I wouldn't any more. Before you go, I hope you do realize that I will never forget what you have done for me today. It was an act of great kindness.

TOPLIS: No no.

[*Looks at her*]

I assure you. It wasn't.

[*He turns away and leaves the room. She watches him go*]

38/1. EXT. THE BLACKWELL FOOTBALL PITCH DAY. THE FOLLOWING DAY

[*Hopefully set beneath the colliery slag heap.*

We see 'the motley crew which marched on to the field to greet the ceremonial drillmaster. Most wear their pit boots, two full-dress uniforms with medals adorning two middle-aged Boer War veterans.

Each man carried the long wooden handle used on miners' shovels or a rifle.' (Further research indicates that a Voluntary Training Corps would also be badged and uniformed to a degree and some would be armed]

TODD: By the left. Quick march. Left right. Left right . . . Parade halt. Left turn.

[*As they arrive in the centre of the field, we see facing them, leaning on his walking stick, with a regal disposition, Captain* TOPLIS. *A crowd flanks the boundary*]

TOPLIS: Parade order arms – stand at ease – stand easy.

[*One man immediately drops his shovel handle*]

Parade 'shun! Parade, right dress. Eyes front. From the right number.

MEN: 1,2,1,2,1, 2, 1,2,1,2.

TOPLIS: Form fours.

[*We see the hopeless muddle and bumping into each other that this order brings. One man turns the wrong way*]

Parade slope arms. Parade right turn. Parade by the left quick march.

[*They stumble around the pitch.* TOPLIS *doesn't allow them to get too far away*]

Left wheel . . . Left wheel . . . Left wheel. Left wheel. Left wheel. Left wheel. Parade halt. Parade will retire. Right turn.

[*They re-approach* TOPLIS. *As they pass in front of him, he sees* TODD *and* JOHNSON *in the ranks*]

Privates Todd and Johnson – three paces forward march! Present arms, slope arms. Left turn. About turn. Left turn. Present arms. Slope arms, order arms.

[*They are now steaming*]

Privates Todd and Johnson, prone position. Down.

[TODD *and* JOHNSON *lie on the ground. Everyone else enjoys the moment*]

Privates Todd and Johnson, Up! Stand at ease.

[TODD *and* JOHNSON *relax, as much as they can*]

Atten-shun – Privates Todd and Johnson! About turn. Charge!

[TODD *and* JOHNSON *go careering through the rest of the men, holding their rifles. No order is given so they keep going. In the end,* JOHNSON, *at the top of a slag heap, throws down his rifle and sits down, wildly out of breath, as well as angry.* TODD *actually keeps going a little longer, till he can go no further, except to climb the slag heap.* TOPLIS *turns at the boundary edge and waves with authority towards the rest of the men in the middle of the field*]

Ah, Parade – Parade dismissed!

[TOPLIS *walks towards the spectators.* FRANK *and* ANNIE *move to him. Laughter and admiration all around*]

FRANK: Y' don't owe me anything now, not a bloody thing . . .

38A/1. INT. PHOTOGRAPHIC STUDIO. DAY

[ANNIE *tidies* TOPLIS *up and goes to stand beside the photographer.*

TOPLIS *is posing for the photograph that will finally be titled 'The most wanted man in Britain' with a certain warm and open-faced conceit.*

ANNIE *nods to the photographer*]

ANNIE: Do you really have to go back next week?

TOPLIS: Aye, but I'm buggered if I will.

[*As* TOPLIS *poses, the light flashes. He continues to take up different poses as the lights flash*]

FADE OUT

EPISODE 2
BEFORE THE SHAMBLES

39/2. EXT. CEMETERY. ROAD TO BULLRING DAWN

[*A blank screen, like a blackout.*

On the bottom of the screen we establish time and place: 'Etaples Base and Training Camp, France. June 1917'.

Light emerging, becoming a sunrise. The sound of bagpipes approaching, warm and stirring and noble.

As this happens, we perhaps see Wilfred Owen's description of Etaples Base Camp on the bottom of the screen:

'Etaples is a vast dreadful encampment, neither France nor England, but a kind of paddock where the beasts are kept a few days before the shambles.' *Wilfred Owen.*

And with the sunrise, we see the cemetery and several WAACs with shovels, tending graves.

The WAACs then march past, part of a Scottish regiment, the Gordons. Quick marching to the bagpipes and through the corridor of insult known as 'The Canary Run'.

'The instructors were lined up five or six feet apart on either side of the road to the bullring. Through the gauntlet of ranting swearing Canaries, the troops passed at the quick march.

'Any man whose rifle was not at the correct slope, whose puttee was loose or unsymmetrical, who had any mark on a uniform, would be swamped in a torrent of oaths.'

As the soldiers go off into the distance, we hear a clatter of a cart and a funeral party of 'professional mourners', a Chaplain, an officer, and coffin bearers.

The cart goes past us]

40/41/2. EXT. BULLRING. MONTAGE. DAY

[*We see the Bullring.*

As many men as possible stand in the centre of it. In almost ridiculous lines, close together, apparently practising the delights of sticking in the bayonet – time after time.

Action abounds around them.

Other men in full kit are jumping up and down to the Canaries' demands.

– Until we reach the bayonet range.

We see, briefly, men in full kit charging with full pack and fixed bayonet across the sand.

They are hounded as they go, physically and verbally, by Canaries free from packs and guns and bayonets, full of food and no fear of the front. They are approaching the stuffed dummies]

WALL-EYE'S MATE: Up, up, up, you bastards, up.

[*And we see* LADY ANGELA FORBES *in one of her ten mobile tea huts.* LADY ANGELA FORBES *is still beautiful at the age of forty-one, wearing the height of summer fashion for the year. If there is something patronizing about her, we also see that she watches the events with a clear sense of misgiving, and finally disgust with the injustice and cruelty that surrounds her. When we focus on her, we also see at one point that she looks towards a car on the roadway above the Bullring, almost but quite deliberately not totally hidden. We can just see a man standing up in the open car, looking at her through binoculars. We return to* LADY FORBES *as she watches the jumping up and down. We see one of the soldiers finally cave in and fall to the ground. Others are near to collapse too, but try to keep going. The* CANARY *with the most unfortunate wall eye approaches the soldier on the ground*]

WALL-EYE: Get up . . . get up . . . you'll be crucified for a week if you don't get up . . . *get up*!

[*The soldier tries to get to his feet. Collapses again. We see* WALL EYE *and another Canary kick and batter the soldier, and finally drag him towards the crucifying posts, where other men are tied up. We see* LADY FORBES *trying to control her anger*]

42/2. EXT. ROADSIDE. BETWEEN ETAPLES AND BOULOGNE. DAY

[TOPLIS, *a draft from the RAMC, plus two or three other drafts, being route-marched along by their own officers.*

They are having their midday rest, where they got half a slice of bread and a mug of water.

TOPLIS *is typically sitting, poker-faced, seemingly unperturbed, at the side of the men, some of whom are already suffering from the first half of the twenty-mile march.*

A couple of men, with obvious blisters, are regretting the experience.

TOPLIS *studies his half slice of bread. There should be something about* TOPLIS *now, somewhat similar to the change in him when he came out of Lincoln Jail after two years hard labour in 1915, that indicates a tiredness and a more withdrawn callousness.*

Battleworn and brutalized without the war.

Unlike many of those around him, fresh-faced young conscripts.

TOPLIS *closes his eyes. Hears a Geordie voice. Opens his eyes, looks up into the sun*]

GEORDIE: Percy Toplis! It is, isn't it?

TOPLIS: Depends who wants to know.

[*Shields his eyes. The* GEORDIE *sits down.* TOPLIS *looks at him coldly*]

Hellfire Corner.

GEORDIE: Right! The autumn of fifteen.

[*Shakes hands as he talks*]

Well I never! So, what've you been up to, Perce?

TOPLIS: Nothing much.

GEORDIE: Why away, man – come on, it's nearly two years. A rum bugger like you'd have done a lot more than nowt much.

TOPLIS [*flatly, staring out*]: Almost went to Mesopotamia. Boat got stopped at Malta when we got beaten to shit in Mesopotamia, spent some time in Malta. Came back. Went absent. Got caught. Sent here.

[*Finally looks at the* GEORDIE]

GEORDIE: See me wound stripe. I got a blighty one.

[GEORDIE *looks for some sympathy, even a reaction. Gets none. Still tries, holds his chest*]

Aye, a bullet nicked a lung, had to send me home . . . they say I'm all right now, more's the pity.

[*Still no reaction*]

. . . Those were good times we had back then.

[TOPLIS *withers him quietly*]

We all missed you, y'know, you an' the Cockney. The bloody tricks you two got up to. It wasn't the same after you left . . . and Jimmy went.

TOPLIS [*viciously*]: Jim's dead. Missin' the bastard won't bring him back.

GEORDIE: Christ, Percy, you an' him were thick as thieves.

TOPLIS: We're not anymore. Are we?

[*Flicks the bread at the* GEORDIE]

Here, do you want that?

[TOPLIS *stands and walks away, looks down the road towards where Etaples will be*]

SERGEANT MARCHER: Get up, get up, let's get goin', you're really going to like it where you're goin' . . . Only twelve miles to go now. Come on. Mummy's waiting for you!

[*We just catch* TOPLIS *turning meanly towards the* SERGEANT. *The soldiers assemble into ranks and march off*]

43/2. EXT. BASE CAMP/FIELD PUNISHMENT AREA. DAY

[*We look towards the field punishment area.*

A soldier is running round with a rifle above his head.

We see and distinctly hear a group of Australian privates surrounding several British Tommies tied in field punishment number one position to a row of posts. The man seen earlier studying LADY FORBES *is watching the scene from the safety of his car. He is Assistant Provost Marshal* STRACHAN. *Another group of Australian officers watch from further away. All are ready for departure, and all drunk. They have found a way to continue drinking both furiously and yet with a certain degree of surreptition. The Australians near to the fence slice through the bonds keeping the wrists of the Tommies strapped to the posts. The first couple of Tommies, when released, drop almost head-first to the floor, till the Australians start to hold them first, and then cut the bonds around their ankles. Drink is inevitably offered to the men – with no surreptition. As this happens, we see a knot of several military policemen, some distance away, on the furthest corner away from* STRACHAN. *The Military Policemen are watching, nervous and undecided. They are outnumbered and aware of what the often physically bigger Australians are capable of doing. We are aware of a reluctant, overweight* SERGEANT, and, much to the fore, a man we will later recognize as Private HARRY REEVE, *the boxing champion and initial cause of the first riot: with a face like a broken plate of beans on toast*]

REEVE: What have we here, then?

MP SERGEANT: I don't fancy it, they don't know what fear is, that crowd . . .

REEVE [*broad Somerset*]: They come near me, they will. I hate Australians.

MP SERGEANT: Best turn a blind eye, Reeve – they're off up the line today. And where they're goin', they won't be comin' back.

[*Another MP coughs and indicates* STRACHAN *watching them. Turns away. They look and see* STRACHAN*'s car, framed in the junction with the top road. He is looking towards them, past the laughing slicing crowd of Australian privates*]

Oh Christ, it's all right for Strachan.

REEVE: Come on.

[*The* SERGEANT *attempting a brave face, sucked in stomach and a swagger, approaches the Australians by the posts, followed by the other MPs*]

MP SERGEANT: You men, what do you think you're doing?

FIRST AUSSIE: What's it to you, fat man?

MP SERGEANT: Stop it now.

SECOND AUSSIE: Pardon?

[*The* SECOND AUSSIE *slashes the bonds on the final wrists and steps back. The Tommy on the fence falls head first, with a thump, his ankles still bound. Sniggers from the Australians*]

Sorry, Tommy.

MP SERGEANT [*glancing towards* STRACHAN]: Tie those men back to the fence . . . Now.

SECOND AUSSIE: Tie them yourself. You put them there.

[*Second* AUSSIE *throws some rope at them. It hits* REEVE *in the face. He steps forward*]

Here, you Tommy Woodbine bastard, you crucify them.

REEVE: You shouldn't ought to have done that.

SECOND AUSSIE [*weighing him up*]: Why, what are you going to do? . . . trench dodger.

[*The other Australians start quietly counting out numbers, an Anzac custom, downwards from ten.* REEVE *draws his baton*]

REEVE: Nobody calls me that.

FIRST AUSSIE: Trench dodger.

[*Before they can finish,* REEVE *is already flying at the* SECOND AUSSIE, *baton waving as they tumble. The fight begins, a scrambling, dusty, ugly brawl – watched by* STRACHAN *from a distance. Also, with interest, by the rest of the Australians, not least the officers. Particularly when the MPs begin to inflict damage with their batons, boots and heavy belts.* REEVE *starts to struggle with his holster for his pistol, and one of the Aussie officers stands up, bottle in hand*]

OFFICER AUSSIE: Gentlemen . . . I think this needs sorting out.

[*Followed by other officers, the officer walks across to the mêlée, and very carefully selects* REEVE *out of the scrum and breaks the bottle over his head, just as* REEVE *releases his gun, and knocks him to the floor*]

44/2. INT. BRIGADIER GENERAL THOMSON'S OFFICE. DAY

[*We see a big, once-muscular, tightly-lipped man, perhaps almost pretty fifty years ago, but now patently gone to seed physically, and not helped any by a small moustache with swirling waxed ends.*

BRIGADIER GENERAL THOMSON *is at his desk, writing. He is surrounded by the maps and graphs and details of his command, and the comforts of his position.*

Here and often there in his office are photographs, pre-war in origin, of officers in full dress uniform.

Happy days.

Nearby, a massive lunch lies in bites about a smallish dining table. STRACHAN *sits pouring out his third port*]

THOMSON: Damned Australians! Wild bad-mannered ill-disciplined rabble.

[STRACHAN *speaks drolly, for he fancies himself to be a gentleman*]

STRACHAN: And that's just the officers.

THOMSON [*snorts*]: The trouble with the Australians, apart from their criminal heritage and natural offensiveness, is quite simply that they have no death penalty. GHQ knows, Haig knows, everyone knows and yet nothing is done about it.

[THOMSON *comes forward to* STRACHAN *for another drink*]

STRACHAN: Anyway they have been –

THOMSON: You cannot win a war without control of your troops, and what control can you have, ultimately, without the death penalty?

STRACHAN: Yes ind –

THOMSON: And it's all very well people telling me how brave they are in battle –

[STRACHAN *waits awhile.* THOMSON *drinks and puts down his glass; he sits.* STRACHAN *begins to pare his fingernails with a penknife*]

STRACHAN: Anyway, they've been attended to by some of my . . . more accomplished men. Don't worry, their arrival at the Front will not be delayed. You're looking tired, Andrew. Are you messing out anywhere special tonight?

THOMSON: Oh, somewhere, I suppose. Guinness knows. Good man Guinness. He'll tell me.

STRACHAN [*rising with difficulty*]: Yes, well I suppose I'd better . . . go and . . .

THOMSON: Yes . . . Yes. Might take a short nap myself.

[*There is a knock at the door*]

Come in.

[GUINNESS, *one of* THOMSON*'s adjutants, comes in with two official-looking lists*]

Ah, Guinness . . .

GUINNESS [*handing a list*]: Arrivals, sir. And drafts for the front line, sir.

[THOMSON *glances at the lists;* GUINNESS *watches him, then possibly enjoys very quietly his next message*]

And if I may remind you, sir, Lady Angela Forbes is still waiting in the outer office.

THOMSON [*gets up*]: Good Lord, I completely . . . Better send the good lady in.

STRACHAN [*smiling*]: Another sermon I expect, I leave you to it, Andrew.

[LADY FORBES *flurries in past* STRACHAN*; stares angrily at* THOMSON]

THOMSON: Ah. Lady Angela . . . very important discussion . . . matters of great importance . . . I'll . . . do please take a seat. Terribly sorry . . . Just see Strachan out.

[*Both men go out.* STRACHAN *closes the door behind them. We focus on* LADY FORBES, *who finds it totally impossible to sit down or still.*

Her impatience burns away. She turns towards the door as they exit and then towards the window, when she hears laughter. She leaves the room and enters the outer office. LADY FORBES *sees a blushing* GUINNESS, *an open door and daylight. She marches towards the open door and looks out*]

44A/2. EXT. THOMSON'S OFFICE. DAY

[*We see two portly, splendidly dressed figures walking away, Army stiff and correct, except that their shoulders are heaving with suppressed laughter and they are struggling slightly to keep in a straight line.*

They march on and on without looking back]

45/2. EXT. BRIDGE/BASE CAMP. DAY

[*We hear The Last Post being played again. And played and played again and again till we don't notice it is there anymore. It just leaks into the scene.*

We see TOPLIS*'s draft passing the bridge into the town near the base camp at Etaples, still at an infantry march.*

We see MPs guarding the bridge and officers crossing into town with WAACs.

We enter the camp. Several men, including a now-coughing GEORDIE, *are staggering behind, to the delight of some of the NCOs, and several lounging Canaries, who are eyeing up potential victims. At the very back, one fat boy is being harried, sworn at and threatened as he stumbles along. We also see the onlookers.*

Anyone who isn't an officer, Instructor or Military Policeman – and there should be a lot of those – has the look expressed by Owen – 'like dead rabbits'.

We see men washing and shaving outside a bath house; sitting at trestle-like tables by the Salvation Army hut and outside a mess tent, washing and shaving; and Aussies queuing up with their billy cans.

Then the Australians we saw earlier, being marched by many MPs, watched by STRACHAN *from his motor car. The Australians approach, limping, bruised and bloody-minded. And quietly, in unison, 'baa-baaing' like sheep, to the absolute hissing rage of some of the MPs*]

AUSTRALIANS: Baa-baa-baa-baa-baa-baa-baa-baa-baa-baa-baa-baa-baa-baa . . .

MPS: Shut up . . . shut up . . . shut up . . . shut up . . . shut up . . .

AUSTRALIANS: Baa-baa-baa-baa-baa-baa-baa-baa-baa-baa-baa-baa-baa-baa-baa-baa . . .

[TOPLIS *breaks stride and half stops, as he continues to look back over his shoulder. This time he is laced into line by a nearby Canary.* TOPLIS *turns threateningly, fists on their way to being raised, but then stops and grins affably and easily. Nearly. He slides immediately, with just the slightest hint of excess, into an immaculate marching step. They are halted near* STRACHAN*'s car in the camp*]

46/2. EXT. BEACH TRENCH. THE BULLRING DAY

[*We see and hear marching again. But now dulled and muddied by sand. It is a hot sunny day – a rare event for the summer of 1917. However:*

'High collars had to stay tightly buttoned, sleeves immaculately rolled down. The soft sand dragged at the ankles. Wet, it strained the khaki of the uniform to the fury of the Canaries. Dry, it penetrated collar and cuff to rasp the flesh against the coarse serge. The soldiers dug at the soft sand. Inevitably, immediately, it trickled back and scorned their efforts.

'The Instructors raged. The sand muffled all sound and made it impossible to keep step. The Instructors savaged the defaulters.'

We see TOPLIS *and as many men as possible piling sandbags in and flailing with shovels at the wet sand, making a trench. Head down, sand going everywhere as they dig, whispering quietly and ironically*]

LANCASHIRE LAD: . . . A trench, they want a piggin' trench on a piggin' beach, has no one ever told them what happens to piggin' sandcastles . . . And what's piggin' more, those piggin' bastards never seen a piggin' trench.

HARD MAN [*throwing down his shovel*]: This is stupid. What happens after we've done this, hey?

TOPLIS: We go over the top into No-Man's Water.

[*The laughter spills out and spreads. The* WALL-EYED CANARY *makes his appearance – he stands above* TOPLIS *and a red-haired soldier as they try to bang the sodden sandbags against the sodden sand at the side of the sodding trench leading to 'No-Man's Water'*]

WALL EYE: Oi, what are you doing? Oi, you lot, what do you think you're doing?

[WALL EYE *believes that he is focusing solely on the 'carrothead' next to* TOPLIS. *At first* TOPLIS *makes a genuine mistake and believes that he is talking to him. But only at first*]

You – I'm talking to you.

TOPLIS: }
CARROTHEAD: } Sergeant!

WALL EYE: Not you – *him*!

TOPLIS: }
CARROTHEAD: } Sorry, Sergeant.

[*They both turn away*]

WALL EYE: You – Carrothead. I'm talking to you.

[CARROTHEAD *moves in front of* TOPLIS *slightly, where he thinks* WALL EYE*'s focus might be*]

Tell me, what are you doing?

CARROTHEAD: We're er . . .

[*Indicates as he peeps out of the trench*]

. . . like putting sandbags in this trench. Sergeant. To fortify it against an attack, Sergeant.

WALL EYE [*to* CARROTHEAD]: What kind of attack?

TOPLIS: Well Sergeant, sorry Sergeant . . .

[TOPLIS *winces most sincerely.* TOPLIS *puts his head down and turns away. We see the rest of the men sniggering like schoolboys in the trench out of sight.* CARROTHEAD *still faces* WALL EYE]

WALL EYE: What kind of attack?

CARROTHEAD: Er . . . er waves. Sergeant, he er . . . said they'd come in waves, Sergeant.

[*Laughs ingratiatingly*]

I've just seen the joke, Sergeant. Waves.

WALL EYE: *It wasn't a joke.*

CARROTHEAD: Oh. Ah. I see. Sorry. Sergeant.

[*We see the tide trickling towards them. Waves are approaching. As* WALL EYE *begins his final speech, we may move down into the trench to see the soldiers and the soaking sandbags, and the look of impotent rage on many of the men's faces. They begin to struggle out of the 'trench' and carry their sandbags*]

WALL EYE: You will be, son, because you and your cronies will pick those sandbags up and you will retire twenty yards to the rear, where you will notice that the sand is dry. Now get up and get moving. Come on. Move it.

[*The soldiers throw some sandbags out of the trench, and* LANCASHIRE LAD *mutters under his breath*]

LANCASHIRE LAD: Piggin' bastard.

47/2. EXT. ASSAULT COURSE. DAY

[*Men are lined up, tied to posts in field punishment number one positions.*

We see TOPLIS *and the other men from the 'trench'.*

The GEORDIE, *looking shattered, has positioned himself near to* TOPLIS]

WALL EYE'S MATE: At the high port, ready, now stick it in them! . . .

[*We see* TOPLIS *keeping in the line for some time*]

WALL EYE: Anybody lagging behind will be on a charge. Come on. Forget you're a white man, stick it in and twist it around. *Stick it in them!* What do you think you're on? An afternoon walk? Now move. Come on.

[*The* GEORDIE *is trying to keep up as well, but begins to drop behind. He falls down. Almost without breaking stride,* TOPLIS *throws him onto his feet and carries on. However,* WALL EYE *and his cohorts are behind them waiting for such a sign of weakness. As the* GEORDIE *goes down the hill he falls against the barbed wire, grazing himself. While the* GEORDIE *falls further and further behind, to be chivvied by other Canaries,* WALL EYE *starts chasing after* TOPLIS *– with some advice*]

. . . Move it, move it, y' leave the fallen behind, lad, he's not a handbag, he's a liability . . . come on, call yourself a soldier, you skinny little runt, didn't they feed you at home . . . your mother too busy was she . . . ? You didn't like that, did you – you don't have to, take it out on Fritz over there, and stick it in him, imagine he's done it to your mother, he would if he could.

[*And finally* TOPLIS, *white-faced throughout, starts screaming and running crazily towards the ridge, leaving the already heaving* WALL EYE *behind.* WALL EYE *turns around to see the* GEORDIE *coming gasping towards him, flanked by two taunting Canaries*]

WALL EYE'S MATE: Come on. Get a move on. Keep that arse down and that muzzle up. Here's the real runt in the litter, the one his mammy should've put down at birth but took pity on . . . come on, mummy's boy . . . that's better . . . no it's not! . . . *faster faster!* Red cross bastard . . . Get up and stick it in him. *Get up, get up!*

[*The* GEORDIE, *on the ground, looks up plaintively*]

GEORDIE: I'm a medic, Sarge. I'm not infantry. And I've just come out of hospital.

WALL EYE: Another bloody malingerer.

[WALL EYE *raps* GEORDIE*'s hand with his swagger stick – not a hard blow but hardly a love tap. The* GEORDIE *slowly rises, using his rifle as support. We still hear screams, but in the distance, as the other men arrive at Fritz and start sticking it into him*]

It's not a walking stick, you useless bugger – it's a rifle, and now it's got a fouled-up barrel. Get up and get going or I'll crucify you to a post till eternity!

[*Again, the* GEORDIE *slowly rises, coughing for his breath, drags himself up, gets his gun, and tries to jump over the water jump. He is 'aided' by one or two Canaries*]

Now there he is, one fat juicy Fritz, run at him, scream at him, tear his heart out an' kill him. Kill him – *kill him*!

[WALL EYE *pushes the* GEORDIE *towards the bayonet range. Everyone is forced to sit and watch. Before he can get kicked this time, the* GEORDIE *gets to his feet and hurtles over the parapet and down towards a sack stuffed and hanging on a frame. He stumbles as he gets there, and ruins the sack's future prospects rather than killing it*]

WALL EYE'S MATE: . . . Friggin' hell, what's the good of shovin' it there – you want to take his life, not his voice.

[WALL-EYE'S MATE *and* GAS CANARY *move towards the* GEORDIE *as he sags desperately against the swinging sack, before slowly sliding down it, and onto the sand. The Canaries pick him up and begin to slide him away.* WALL EYE *reaches them at a leisurely pace*]

WALL EYE: Oh no, play fair, men. Don't put him on a charge. We'll give him another chance.

GAS CANARY: All right, Sarge.

WALL EYE: In fact we'll give him lots of chances – on your feet. You and all your mates back to the beginning. Now!

[*The two lesser Canaries drag the* GEORDIE *towards the field punishment area. We see* TOPLIS *and the others in line. In silence. Disbelief is registered on the faces of those who are having their first sample of the sadism. As* TOPLIS *and the others watch the* GEORDIE *staggering to his feet they inevitably speak in harsh whispers. They get up and move off*]

CARROTHEAD: . . . What do you write home after today? Hey?

LANCASHIRE LAD: Nothing. 'Cos they wouldn't piggin' well believe you.

CARROTHEAD: . . . What a bad war it is here.

HARD MAN [*with absolute intent*]: I'm going to kill that bastard Canary before I leave.

[*We see* TOPLIS *look at the* HARD MAN *out of the corner of his eye. Previously expressionless to the point of disinterest as he waits in line, he now glances back towards the approaching* WALL EYE, *and a mean smile finally slips out – as if he too is thinking of how he would set about it*]

48/2. INT/EXT. THE GAS HUT
LATER THAT DAY

[*A darkened wooden hut of some size. Full of sand, and various gases at various times – chlorine would produce a green/yellow haze. Two pairs of curtains contain the gas inside the hut.*

We see the HARD MAN *being released from the gas hut. He staggers out, coughing.*

We see outside. Most of the men have gone through, and have been allowed to sit and recover. Only the GEORDIE *is left for the experience of a lifetime.*

The men who have got through sit on a small ridge, watching the GEORDIE.

Several of them are mumbling and debating together.

TOPLIS *is one of them.*

As the GEORDIE *is next, the* HARD MAN *returns and goes towards the gas hut, stepping in front of a Canary*]

GAS CANARY: Next.

HARD MAN: He's not going.

GAS CANARY: Who says so?

HARD MAN: I do.

GAS CANARY: Who are you?

[*Shouts*]

Sar'nt!

HARD MAN: The bloke who's just told you he isn't going. He's not fit.

GAS CANARY: Oh I see, a doctor in disguise.

[*The* LANCASHIRE LAD *stands up. As he does so,* WALL EYE

approaches and takes in the scene and taking off his cap. Three other Canaries join him]

LANCASHIRE LAD: None of us want him to go. He's ill, any fool can see that.

WALL EYE: . . . Anyone else share those views?

[*Slowly the lot of them stand up, and face out silently.* TOPLIS *is the last to stand*]

Well then, let's see if I can't change your minds for you.

[WALL EYE *smiles at them, then turns around and, without any warning whatsoever, butts the* HARD MAN *in the face. As the* HARD MAN *slumps to the floor,* WALL EYE *steps briskly away from the scene. The* HARD MAN *is descended upon by the other Canaries in a vile flurry of boots. As he slumps unconscious he is dragged away by the arms.* WALL EYE *turns to the standing men – except that they have all sat down. The* LANCASHIRE LAD *is in the act of sitting down, the last of all. They all look away – except* TOPLIS]

WALL EYE: You were saying, gentlemen . . .?

[*Looks to the Gas Canaries at the front of the gas hut*]

GAS CANARY: *Next.*

[WALL EYE *pushes the* GEORDIE *into the gas hut*]

LANCASHIRE LAD: Thanks for your support, lads.

[TOPLIS *only speaks when no one else does*]

TOPLIS: That's not the way. Y' don't play fair with those bastards.

[*The* LANCASHIRE LAD *looks at him. So do a few others.* TOPLIS *looks towards the* HARD MAN *being dragged across the sand by his arms. Then looks towards the* GEORDIE *as he is bounced into the gas hut*]

. . . You play the game the way they play it . . .

[TOPLIS *finally looks at the* LANCASHIRE LAD]

Without any rules.

[*We move away from the scene. As we do so, we see that, unbeknown to the men, at a point behind them, higher and further away,* LADY ANGELA FORBES *has been watching. We reach her as she turns and moves out of sight, in a flurry of sand, anger and elbows*]

49/50/2. INT. THOMSON'S OFFICE. DAY

[*The door is opened by* GUINNESS. *A* CORPORAL CLERK *is in the corner of the room, taking notes.*]

GUINNESS: Lady Angela Forbes.

[LADY FORBES *flourishes in.* THOMSON *is standing behind his desk;* STRACHAN, *sitting at the side of it, has not got up.* LADY FORBES *glares at* STRACHAN. *He stands up, penknife in hand.*]

FORBES: Before we commence, I would prefer Strachan to leave the room. Thank you, Captain Strachan.

[STRACHAN *looks up with genteel surprise*]

THOMSON: Lady Angela, Assistant Provost Marshal Strachan is –

FORBES: Would you go Captain Strachan. And take your penknife with you.

STRACHAN: General?

[THOMSON *nods, dismissing* STRACHAN. STRACHAN *nods*]

STRACHAN: I shall see you soon enough, no doubt, Lady Angela. Here and there. As we go our merry rounds.

[STRACHAN *departs.* THOMSON *leans forward as he goes, solicitously. Lifts a cigarette box towards* LADY FORBES]

THOMSON: Do please take a seat.

[*She sits*]

A cigarette, Lady Angela? Perhaps a whisky and soda?

[LADY FORBES *barely contains her anger. Now that she has sat, the* CORPORAL CLERK *does likewise*]

FORBES: I rarely smoke in public, General, or indeed in private, and I never drink before dinner, let alone luncheon. As you well know.

THOMSON: My apologies. You just seemed a trifle . . . flurried, ma'am.

[*Smiles*]

FORBES [*smiling back*]: Flurried, what a quaint word . . .

[*Sharply*]

I am not flurried, General, I am downright bloody angry!

THOMSON [*to* CORPORAL CLERK]: I trust that comment has been minuted, Matthews.

[*The* CORPORAL CLERK *nods as he takes notes*]

Including the profanity?

[*The* CORPORAL CLERK *nods again, avoiding looking at either of them*]

I am so sorry, do please continue.

FORBES: I have just come from the Bullring –.

THOMSON [*to* CORPORAL CLERK]: Training Camp Number One, Matthews, not 'Bullring'.

FORBES: – where I was forced to witness –

THOMSON: I do not think you were . . .

[FORBES *holds her hand up to stop the interruption*]

FORBES: – where I had the opportunity to witness your so-called instructors performing forms of humiliation and cruelty usually associated with a minor inquisition and I really feel –

THOMSON: Just one minute please, Lady Angela. We have investigated these complaints before. You have, if you recall, corresponded with me on the subject and then saw fit to communicate your ill-advised observations not only to my superiors at General Headquarters, but seemingly to half of London Society.

[*He glints at* LADY FORBES]

Do we really need to waste any more of your valuable time on these . . . trivialitics?

FORBES: Your so-called instructors are one step away from being inhuman.

THOMSON: I train men to go into battle, you serve tea at midday on the training ground. I do not question the quality of your tea, I have never once asked if it were Darjeeling or Ceylon.

[*Pause*]

FORBES: The men believe that the only reason the Canaries –

THOMSON [*sharply*]: Instructors. Delete 'Canaries'.

FORBES [*turning sharply*]: Would you care to delete my previous 'bloody' as well?

[*Turns back*]

I will have a cigarette, damn you.

[*Back to* CORPORAL CLERK, *pleasantly*]

D.A.M.N.

[*She reaches out for a cigarette, takes one, and holds it as if she is expecting it to be lit for her.* THOMSON *manages to lean back ever so slightly.* LADY FORBES *puts the cigarette back and closes the box, as* THOMSON *talks*]

THOMSON: Now . . . is there any other issue that I could assist you with. Ma'am.

[LADY FORBES *rises and stands facing* THOMSON *across the desk*]

FORBES: Very well. Before I take this matter any further I must again ask you whether or not you intend to remove Assistant Provost Marshal Strachan from this camp.

[THOMSON *closes his eyes for some time*]

THOMSON: For what reason, Lady Angela?

[*Opens his eyes*]

FORBES [*patiently, but with difficulty*]: Have you not seen how Strachan's Military Police . . . 'perform their duties' in Etaples?

THOMSON: *I know that all efforts are made to keep discipline, ma'am.* I am equally certain that Assistant Provost Marshal Strachan, being responsible for the Military Police, supervises with considerable success the maintenance of that discipline.

FORBES: I would go as far as to say that you are sitting on a powder keg.

[THOMSON *looks down at his chair. Carefully*]

THOMSON: Would you care to substantiate that ridiculous statement?

[*As* LADY FORBES *continues, she reaches a climax, that is, in her anger, not far short of hysterical/theatrical.* THOMSON*'s reply too, should be truthfully big. Few holds barred between these two. Like the best of Hepburn and O'Toole in 'The Lion in Winter'. And I think that the scene will only carry and work if played this way. So there*]

FORBES: Certainly. Every day, young men who will probably have to lay down their lives for their country are being treated like livestock instead of heroes. Either brutalized in the Bullring by mindless thugs or penned up like cattle in their depots. They are not even allowed to visit the town, whilst NCOs and officers come and go as they please. I complain about these appalling conditions and what happens? Men who stop and talk to me in confidence are followed and questioned by Strachan's military police. They intercept my servants in the street and question them about the identity of my weekend guests. Strachan follows me in his motor car for no other reason than to intimidate me, and when I have the dubious pleasure of being in his company, he does nothing less than leer at me while paring his fingernails with a penknife!

THOMSON: Oh well then, of course, the man must go.

[*He leans forward, his turn to fly*]

Lady Angela, forgive me if I speak plainly. I know that you know socially Lord Derby, members of the Royal Family and generals at the War Office. I acknowledge your easy popularity with the rank and file. The fame of your charitable work goes before you. But – you are a civilian. And a woman to boot.

FORBES: As usual, Thomson, you are able to make a compliment sound like an insult.

[THOMSON *rises and leans across his desk to* LADY FORBES]

THOMSON: The insult, madam, is that you do not understand that this is the greatest conflict mankind has ever experienced. That we must win this war or perish. That my job is to train an army that *can* win this war. And what do they send me? A rabble of wounded men and raw conscripts – the dregs of our cities and the scum of our shires. And our Colonies.

[*We catch the look of disgust on the* CORPORAL CLERK*'s face.* THOMSON *has gone too far*]

FORBES: I hope and trust that will be accurately minuted, Corporal.

51/2. INT. TOPLIS'S TENT. NIGHT

[*Candlelight.*

TOPLIS *is in his tent (twenty-two men to a tent) in one of the base depots.*

He is alone apart from a couple of men some distance away from him, lying on their beds chatting.

TOPLIS *is sitting on the floor between beds.*

He is just completing the making of a 'thud' – a sand-bag cosh. 'Improvised from the white linen ration bags, with just sufficient sand placed in the bag, which is screwed and tied tightly.'

Task completed, we see him apply burnt cork to his face in a rough and ready manner, smearing it all around, and then slipping under the canvas of the bell tent and away]

52/2. EXT. BASE CAMP. NIGHT

[*The same night.*

We see WALL EYE *and a compatriot staggering across the bridge from Etaples, past the guards and on.*

They approach some rows of very similar huts. With very similar gaps between them. We hear them as they approach.

The COMPATRIOT SERGEANT *is singing*]

WALL EYE: Now it's best when you pay, oh yes, give the mademoiselle ten francs, she has no hold then, no hold at all, you just bury the red feller and off you go, well satisfied . . .

COMPATRIOT SERGEANT [*even more obviously drunk*]: The one I was with had nice eyes, Sarge. She had big blue eyes.

WALL EYE: *Are you being funny?*

COMPATRIOT SERGEANT: What? Sarge?

WALL EYE: Nice eyes! I hate nice eyes. It's Baxter, isn't it – you little snot – what's wrong with my eyes?

[COMPATRIOT *fading away into the shadows*]

COMPATRIOT SERGEANT: Er nothin', an' I'm not Baxter, whoever he is – I'm . . . We just met, I'm er. I'm going this way . . . I go this way. I'll see you again then.

[*He goes off. As all this happens, as the two men approach the distinctly similar huts with the distinctly similar gaps, we see a blacked-up* TOPLIS *emerging from one of the gaps. He comes briefly into the light, looks down the line of huts towards the two men, sees* WALL EYE *being left by his compatriot, and tucks into the darkness provided by the shadows in the gaps between huts. We follow* WALL EYE *as he walks on. We see him from a back view as he approaches and passes two or three huts and gaps, breaking wind and muttering*]

WALL EYE: I had a nice nose. Once. Nobody ever talks about that . . .

[*At which point, out of the shadows in the gap between two of the huts, we see the silhouette of an arm and a cosh raised and then brought down savagely across the back of* WALL EYE*'s head as he falls forward. We see that* WALL EYE *is pulled almost totally into the shadows and systematically and brutally beaten. We move down the line of huts towards the scene, see the shadows of the two men and the beating being inflicted almost silently, and horribly. But we can also see, at the same time, the end of the hut and the gap between that and the next hut. Slowly, cautiously, we see a second figure peeping out of the gap and around the hut, watching and listening, till the beating stops and the cosh is thrown down. And we hear footsteps hurrying away down the gap. We see the second figure move furtively towards where* WALL EYE *lies still. We finally see that it is* TOPLIS, *beaten to the punch, looking down at* WALL EYE. *He looks at his cosh, goes to throw it down, then stops. Finally he laughs, before turning down the gap and running quietly away*]

53/2. INT. TOPLIS'S TENT. NIGHT

[*A noisy game of cards in progress. Featuring the* CARROTHEAD, *the* LANCASHIRE LAD, *the* HARD MAN *and* TOPLIS]

TOPLIS: Who's light?

HARD MAN: I'm in.

LANCASHIRE LAD: I'm in.
CARROTHEAD: Oh, it's me.

[*Most of the men are in the tent, some dozing, reading, writing. A quieter game of crown and anchor amongst the intellectuals goes on in another part of the tent. The* HARD MAN *still bears clear signs of the beating at the feet of the Canaries, and his wrists are red raw from the rope of his field punishment.* TOPLIS *glances at him as they play brag and ad-lib their way through the game amidst the following conversation*]

CARROTHEAD: So where's the Geordie then?
LANCASHIRE LAD: All I know is they kicked him out the piggin' hospital.
TOPLIS: Oh aye. What the doctor say – 'coughin' blood's good for you'?
LANCASHIRE LAD: You know the rigmarole with the piggin' doctors.
CARROTHEAD: 'Bad teeth, doctor.'
TOPLIS [*affected*]: 'I don't want you to eat the Germans, private.'
CARROTHEAD: 'Consumption, doctor.'
TOPLIS: 'Oh good, you can go and spit at them then.'

[*Laughter*]

CARROTHEAD: If he isn't in hospital where is he?
TOPLIS: I expect he's gone to the seaside.

[*He leans towards the* HARD MAN]

You've got a bit of dirt there, Franny – no there.

[TOPLIS *reaches out and picks at it, just beneath the* HARD MAN*'s eye, then sniffs his fingers. He still watches the* HARD MAN. *The* HARD MAN *looks away.* TOPLIS *looks towards the others*]

LANCASHIRE LAD: I'll see you.

[TOPLIS *shows his hand: an Ace, King and Queen. Scoops the pennies up, looks around, enjoys the moment*]

54/2. INT. FORBES'S CANTEEN. EVENING

[*Five to eight. At eight o'clock it is closed.*

People are already drifting out as they finish their tea and snacks.

Military policemen are watching out especially for secret drinking – serious drinking – as a couple of bottles of spirits make the rounds well wrapped.

We see TOPLIS, *the* GEORDIE *and two strangers, sitting at a table in a corner. The two strangers have their backs turned to the door.*

The first stranger carries a kit bag, and when he speaks he will have a very occasional stammer. They are both in Privates' uniforms – the one on the ill-at-ease second stranger is slightly ill-fitting]

GEORDIE: It's bloody marvellous, Percy. It's safe, man.

TOPLIS: So that's where you been hiding yourself, is it? Well, well, well.

GEORDIE: Honest, Perce, I couldn't take it anymore, and I'm not kidding, it's a bloody paradise compared with here.

TOPLIS: You two got anything to say for yourselves?

STRANGER: I have – he hasn't.

[*The* MP SERGEANT *and another MP enter the canteen*]

MP SERGEANT: All right, all right, all right, you lot should know by now – eight o'clock, Lady Angela's got a home to go to, even if you haven't, off you pop – and take the stink of rum with you. Woe betide y' if I catch y' – if you don't have a pass into town, it's because you don't deserve one.

GEORDIE [*excited*]: I met them in hospital the other day – queueing up for dinner, been doin' it for three days, the pair of them –

STRANGER: Lower your voice, will you?

TOPLIS: And pass the bottle.

[*The* GEORDIE *slides a wrapped-up rum bottle under the table*]

GEORDIE [*more suitably hushed*]: I wondered why one of them was nice as pie and the other one never opened his mouth. Found out, didn't I – this one's a bloody Frenchie.

STRANGER: Look, we're late, we've stayed to impress your friend, now are you coming or not?

MP SERGEANT: *You* – yes, you –

[STRANGER *and the* FRENCHMAN *freeze and slowly look round*]

– come here! And bring y' water bottle with you.

[*A Private stands and approaches the two MPs red-faced and red-handed*]

STRANGER [*quietly*]: Let's get out of here.

GEORDIE: Come on, Perce. *Come on*. It's what they say it is – it's a sanctuary.

[*We see the red-faced soldier standing in front of the MPs*]

MP SERGEANT [*sweetly*]: Breathe on me.

[*The soldier has to lean up on tip toes. And he breathes. The MP affects shock, takes the bottle in the bag and passes it to the second*

MP, then, smiling happily, hurtles the soldier out of the door. As he goes]

Nothing like a bit of Field Punishment to sober up a drunk.

GEORDIE: Well?

[TOPLIS *sees the grim faces and the anger of the men around them. He hands the rum bottle back to the* GEORDIE]

TOPLIS: I'll take the evening air with you, Alfred old boy . . . but that's all.

GEORDIE: Perce. Y' three days away from a train journey.

TOPLIS: I know. Anyway I think I'll stay. I mean, this is no way to go out on the town.

[*He goes out of the doorway. He whistling 'The Marseillaise'. The* FRENCHMAN *is not amused*]

55/2. EXT. THE BEACH/SANCTUARY WOODS NIGHT

[*Woods on one side, water on the other.*
TOPLIS, *the* GEORDIE, *the* TWO STRANGERS]

GEORDIE: You know, I've learnt so much, Perce, just by listening . . .

TOPLIS: Well, it does make a change from talking.

GEORDIE: I know. Just in two days, the things I've found out. Like politics.

TOPLIS: It's completed your education really, being a deserter, hasn't it?

GEORDIE: Yeah.

[*An upset silence from the* GEORDIE]

STRANGER: Well, Alfie said you were a cynic . . .

TOPLIS: A cynic!

STRANGER: But there's many reasons for deserting. And you never know, education could be one of them.

TOPLIS: A reluctance to get killed must come high on the list.

STRANGER: Aye it does, as well as a reluctance to kill your own kind.

TOPLIS [*smiles*]: Germans?

STRANGER [*shakes his head*]: Young men. Cannon-fodder, just like you and me.

TOPLIS: Listen. If you're talking politics, talk to someone else with your grammar school ideas. It's politics got us into this sodding mess.

STRANGER: And it's politics that'll get us out. The politics of socialism.

[*Shrugs*]

I'm a socialist.

TOPLIS: But of course, I mean, aren't we all . . .

STRANGER: And, after being conscripted into this madness, I'm a pacifist as well.

TOPLIS [*flatly*]: I had an uncle who collected stamps . . .

[*The* FRENCHMAN *whistles like a bird as they approach the trees. A whistle is returned.* TOPLIS *smiles sardonically. We see shadows and figures emerge from the trees, and approach*]

FIRST SHADOW: You're late.

STRANGER: We waited for someone. Who wasn't worth waiting for.

[TOPLIS *slaps his own wrist, we hear a low groan of pain from the trees. They all glance over*]

GEORDIE: You'll be all right.

FIRST SHADOW: But did you get the stuff?

[*The* STRANGER *slaps his haversack as they move towards the groans. We follow them a few yards till we see a deserter with a flesh wound in the thigh, lying on a makeshift bed of canvas. We see the* STRANGER *take medical supplies out of the bag. The* GEORDIE *takes hold of them and begins to treat the deserter.* TOPLIS *bends down, without fuss nor favour, and begins to assist*]

TOPLIS: Where did you get these?

STRANGER: From the hospital. We made an unexpected return visit. A sort of surprise.

TOPLIS: Very nice of them to help out like this.

STRANGER: Yes it was rather, wasn't it. Generous, in fact. We even . . . erm 'received' a most pleasant packed lunch.

[*He reveals food from the bottom of the bag*]

TOPLIS [*glancing up*]: Oh how kind.

STRANGER: Well, we had to help ourselves a little, here and there.

TOPLIS: Of course. As I was saying – if that's what socialism is, we're all socialists.

[*A sly grin on* TOPLIS*'s face as he tends to the wounded man*]

That's right, isn't it, Stranger?

STRANGER [*laughs*]: Not really, but you nearly got the name right.

TOPLIS [*as he works*]: What name?

STRANGER: You called me 'Stranger'.

TOPLIS: So?
STRANGER: My name's Strange.
TOPLIS: How strange?
STRANGER: No, Strange. Charles Strange.
TOPLIS: How . . . fascinating.
GEORDIE: Stay here, hey, Perce. Stay here. It's safe here.
TOPLIS: Oh is it?

[*to the* PATIENT]

Did you hear that? It's safe here.

GEORDIE: There's thousands of us all over these woods, we help each other . . .

TOPLIS: I'd rather help meself. No, I think I'll take my chances up the line.

[GEORDIE *puts a piece of wood in the man's mouth to prevent him from biting his tongue*]

But maybe some other time . . .

[*to* WOUNDED MAN]

Now this is going to hurt, hold tight now, as the actress said . . .

[*The* WOUNDED MAN *groans as quietly as he can*]

56/2. EXT. TRENCH. ARRAS. DAY
LATE AUGUST 1917

[TOPLIS *is at the front. In a trench, in the middle of the usual carnage and disgusting bedlam, and in a similar position to that in the previous scene: bent over a wounded but small and very young soldier.*

This time the blood is galloping from the wounded man's thigh.

TOPLIS *briefly tries to staunch the blood and shouts for a stretcher*]

TOPLIS: *Stretcher! Stretcher!* You hang on, Tiny.

[*We see* TOPLIS *leave him and scuttle away towards another wounded and screaming little man. We see that the trench is awash with liquid mud*]

Stretcher bearers.

[*We return to the first wounded soldier and see that he is now dead*]

57/2. EXT. RUINED FARMYARD/CEMETERY BEHIND THE LINES. DUSK/NIGHT

[*We see* TOPLIS *and his fellow stretcher bearers.*
Deathly silence. Shoulders slumped. Carrying bodies to a huge pile at the edge of a cemetery]

58/2. EXT. RUINED FARMYARD AND BATH-HOUSE. DAWN

[*Very early morning. Near the cemetery.*
We see TOPLIS *and his fellow stretcher bearer in the courtyard of a large farm.*
TOPLIS *is sitting against a door to one of the buildings. It is a makeshift casualty clearing station.*
Doctors and various members of the Medical Corps are sitting around, exhausted.
Another building, across the courtyard, equally makeshift, is a small officers' bath-house.
A small Corporal, GILZEAN, *is cleaning a boot just outside the bath-house.*
TOPLIS *looks on.*
His partner is drinking water he has poured from the square petrol cans used for water supplies at the front]

RAMC FELLOW: I wish they'd fix that water pump, I could run a motorbike on the petrol that's still in here.
TOPLIS [*flatly*]: I know, you sound just like a damned two stroke in the mornings.

[*Some bitter laughter from those who have heard* TOPLIS. *It stops as they see a Corporal and two very young Bantam Privates marching through the courtyard, under guard of some of their fellow Bantams and a tall Captain. We see everyone looking at them while attempting not to look at them – except for* TOPLIS, *who looks straight at them*]

RAMC FELLOW: Christ! Here comes another Court Martial.
TOPLIS: What's this for – failure to grow under strict orders?
RAMC FELLOW: Do you really want to know?
TOPLIS: No. But it all helps.

RAMC FELLOW: They ate their iron rations when they were stuck in No Man's Land.

TOPLIS: I thought it'd be something serious.

[*The Bantams are escorted past, and* GILZEAN *stands briefly at the door to the Quartermaster's store, then goes in*]

Well. That just about does it, I reckon. See you, Tom.

[TOPLIS *puts his hand up as he talks. Takes the long bolt out of the lock of the door. It vaguely resembles the barrel of a gun*]

RAMC FELLOW: What do you mean?

TOPLIS: I mean toodleoo. And you haven't seen me.

[*Flatly*]

I'm going back to Etaples.

RAMC FELLOW: Oh hey, it's as bad there as it is here.

TOPLIS [*walking away*]: Not where I'm going.

[TOPLIS *moves towards door of the bath-house and looks through the window*]

59/2. INT. OFFICERS' BATH-HOUSE. DAY

[TOPLIS *crosses the courtyard towards the bath-house, the bolt in his hand.*

He enters the bath-house apparently casually, but as he opens the door his actions increase sharply.

We see TOPLIS *inside the bath-house. Officers' uniforms are laid out and on hooks. Perhaps the sound of someone singing flatly and mournfully from the actual bathing area.*

We see GILZEAN *bent over several pairs of officers' boots, polishing them, spit and all.*

TOPLIS *approaches him quickly, the bolt in his hand. He sticks the bolt in* GILZEAN*'s back, puts his hand around* GILZEAN*'s neck from the back*]

TOPLIS [*quietly*]: Get up. Don't turn around. Nothing will happen if you don't turn around.

GILZEAN [*although scared*]: Y' must be desperate for a bath.

[TOPLIS *puts his hand hard over* GILZEAN*'s mouth, half smiling*]

TOPLIS: I want more than a bath, Jock, I want *four* officers' uniforms, *now*, nothing less than a captain, nothing from your regiment of dwarfs, and one has to be five foot nine – *I said don't turn around.* Then all you have to do is pack them for me. Very neatly. And very fast.

[*A gunfire burst not too far away.* GILZEAN *jumps*]

Yes. I know, I know. Now don't turn around.

[*He pushes* GILZEAN *towards the officers' uniforms, and then moves to where he can cover the entrance to the bathing area, while still seeing out of a window. We see* GILZEAN *manically struggling to fit the uniforms into a valise.* GILZEAN, *his back still turned, speaks plaintive and Glaswegian if that combination is possible*]

GILZEAN: . . . I can't fit them all in.

TOPLIS: *Try.*

GILZEAN: I have. And they won't.

[GILZEAN *half turns round*]

TOPLIS: Don't turn around. And don't be stupid.

GILZEAN: You would na' by any chance be needin' a batman would ye? Sir?

[TOPLIS *weighs him up. We hear officer's voice, slightly imperious, from the bathing area*]

WASHED OFFICER [O.O.V.]: Corporal!

[GILZEAN *turns towards the bathing area instinctively – sees* TOPLIS. *Looks down towards a crammed valise. Moves an open empty valise towards himself and the unpacked officers' uniforms. Silence – as* TOPLIS *weighs him up. The door to the officers' wash area rattles. We hear the* WASHED OFFICER*'s voice again*]

Corporal! What's wrong with this damned door?

[GILZEAN *looks nervously at* TOPLIS]

GILZEAN: It – it's stuck sir. Just one wee minute, sir.

60/2. EXT. COUNTRYSIDE. NEAR PARIS PLAGE DAY

[TOPLIS, *in a Captain's uniform.*

Alongside him, his batman, GILZEAN.

We see two people on horseback approaching them. LADY FORBES *and* GENERAL ASSER]

GILZEAN: Maybe I could have one of the uniforms altered, you know, find a Frenchie tailor in the village, slip him a few francs.

TOPLIS [*as an officer*]: I'm sorry, Gilzean, but you could never be an officer; you have neither the temperament, the accent, the size nor the savoir faire. Stand still.

[TOPLIS *salutes as* ASSER *and* FORBES *ride past – smartly*]

TOPLIS: You are, in short, a small man from Scotland with one stripe. And call me 'Sir' in future.

GILZEAN: Ah go and blacken your bum.

TOPLIS: Ah yes, now there you are, that would go down well in the Officers' Mess. 'And what would your solution be, Gilzean?'

[*Scottish*]

'I don't know, Brigadier, but why don't you go and blacken your bum?'

[*Changes mood and accent as the* CORPORAL *laughs*]

What made all you stunted little sods come here in the first place? You're mad – the size of you lot, you didn't have to fight.

GILZEAN: Aye well, when you're five-foot nothing, you're always lookin' for a fight.

TOPLIS: Yes, but how many do you win?

[*A motor car approaches, with seemingly only a female driver in the car. She glances at an appreciative* TOPLIS *as the car dawdles past.* TOPLIS *then sees a figure slumped and huddled in a corner, looking away.* TOPLIS *turns and watches. And as* TOPLIS *and* GILZEAN *walk on, we follow the car, and we see that the figure is* STRACHAN]

61/2. EXT. COUNTRY ROAD. NEARBY. DAY

[*We see* ASSER *and* FORBES *continuing their horseride – and argument*]

FORBES: All you're saying, Johnnie – your philosophy is – well – it's – it's like people were saying in San Francisco a few years ago – they were probably saying there's never been a major earthquake here – so there never will be one.

ASSER: People do have the strangest conversations . . .

FORBES: Fine – but the Czar of Russia probably had the same illusions about revolutions until the start of this year. It's all very well for you chaps sitting up at GHQ, but you're out of touch. You don't understand how the men feel, stuck here in Etaples, being bullied to death, waiting to go to the Front to be . . .

ASSER: Killed to death? But they still come, granted they are mostly conscripts now but *they still come*. And then they go. With barely a whimper for the most part.

FORBES: But for how long? Etaples will explode, it will, and soon. It's not only the men in the camp, it's all those Bolsheviks and deserters in the sanctuaries.

ASSER: Deserters and cowards don't start revolutions, Angela. And the English don't care enough. Not the lower classes anyway. Otherwise they wouldn't allow themselves to die. For King and Country and Empire.

[*He shrugs*]

The thing is, I believe in King and Country and . . .

FORBES: So do I. And I don't want a revolution. After all, I *know* His Majesty, and members of my family own a substantial part of the country. I'm not a fool. Nor a troublemaker. It's Strachan and Thomson who are the real fools and troublemakers.

[*She glances to her side*]

And if we cut across this hill, we'll lose Strachan completely and be home in time for dinner.

[*She spurs on her horse and they canter over the hill*]

ASSER [*grins*]: Provided, of course, there's no revolution before seven fifteen.

FORBES [*as they go*]: Oh we generally dine later than that . . .

[STRACHAN*'s car draws up and he watches them through his binoculars*]

62/2. EXT. SANCTUARY. WOODS. DAY

[*Establishing shot.*

Pleasure, envy and the magic of 'uniforms'.

We see the STRANGER, FRANCIS *the* HARD MAN *and* GILZEAN, *in the first thrill of being dressed as officers.*

Other members of the sanctuary are watching them. From various vantage points. Trees, dugouts, lying on mattresses etc. GILZEAN *is being jeered in his excess uniform. Cries of 'Charlie Chaplin'*]

GILZEAN: Ach away to – Chuck it –

[GILZEAN *does a Chaplinesque walk in his uniform*]

FIRST SHADOW: When the moon shines bright on Charlie Chaplin
His boots are cracking
For want of blacking,
And his little baggy trousers
They want mending,
Before we send him to the Dardenelles.

[TOPLIS *produces the officers' papers to go with each uniform. Passes the* GEORDIE, *still in private's uniform; looking ill*]

TOPLIS: You sure you're not coming?
GEORDIE: No, I'm not up to it.
TOPLIS: Suit yourself . . . [TOPLIS *reaches the* HARD MAN. *Grins at him as he offers the papers*]
It's good to see you, Franny. You never did see eye to eye with authority, did you.
Now, d'you think you can remember this, Franny – 'Sebastian Blennah-Hassett'.
[TOPLIS *sees* GILZEAN *in the fourth uniform, looking ridiculous and desperate in an officer's jacket far too large for him*]
Take it off, Gilzean, unless you're auditioning for the music hall.
[*As* GILZEAN *sulks out of his jacket,* TOPLIS *glances around. He is standing by the* STRANGER]
One more volunteer for the Etaples tour. Sorry, no Frenchies nor Russian Revolutionaries – if you're going to town with me, you've got to speak English –
[*Glances at the* STRANGER *as he gives him the officer's papers*]
And use small words.
[*He does up one of the* STRANGER*'s buttons*]
Yes, a natural leader of men . . . comrade.

63/2. EXT. SHORELINE. SANCTUARY NO. 1 NIGHT

[*We see* TOPLIS, *the* HARD MAN, *the* STRANGER *and someone else returning from their night in Etaples along the shoreline towards the trees and the 'sanctuary'. They are carrying supplies*]

STRANGER: What other way is there? Born poor, die poor – no alternative. That's the class system, Perce, and you can't fight it totally on your own. You have to have socialism.
TOPLIS: Do I? Who says? Is there a rule book on the subject? 'The Beliefs of Percy Toplis'.
[*Imitates the* STRANGER, *slight stutter and all*]
'Here you are, Percy, my boy.' 'Oh thank you, Stranger, and what are these?' 'These are your beliefs, and go forth and believe.'
[*Spits on the sand*]
Bullshit . . .
[*They enter the wooded area, walking towards the sanctuary*]

STRANGER: So all you care about –

TOPLIS: Listen – *I don't care* – it's as simple as that. Now just leave it alone. 'Cos we had a good night tonight, right?

[*The* STRANGER *nods*]

You got the supplies you wanted. I made a few bob at cards, and we're still alive. Right?

[STRANGER *nods again*]

Right. Well that'll do me. And if I could get a grip on that Mademoiselle we saw tonight that'd do me even better –

STRANGER: The trouble with that attitude –

[*We hear a sudden gunshot from too near for comfort. A quick scream of pain, more shouting.* HARD MAN *turns to* TOPLIS]

HARD MAN: Shut up!

[*As he speaks, we see what appear to be the headlights of several cars suddenly light up an area ahead of them, slightly to one side and also below them. We see the car headlights, the Military Police – all 'brass hats and revolvers flashing' – some lounging about the cars, others marching towards the lights. We see the scene from a height. As the scene continues, we also see that it is the viewpoint of* TOPLIS *and the other three. We see the* GEORDIE *being battered and frogmarched towards the cars. We see another man being hauled along. Trousers around ankles. Finally, we see the small Corporal,* GILZEAN, *with a flesh wound in his arm.* GILZEAN *is being bounced and thrown. And we see* TOPLIS *and the others slide away silently*]

MP: What are you doing, little man?

GILZEAN: Jesus Christ, watch my arm. You bastards, you've shot my arm.

MP: Never mind your arm. You'll get worse where you're going.

64/2. EXT. SANCTUARY. WOODS. DAWN

[*The woods, near the sea.*

Men on look-out on the edge of the group – those that are left. Plus others from another 'sanctuary', who look half drowned. Still a large number of men there.

VERY WET MAN: Our group lost a lot more than you. Bloody dozens. They near enough surrounded us. It's a good job the tide was in.

DESERTER: Bloody good job we could swim as well.

FIRST SHADOW: Well, what do we do now – they'll be shot.

TOPLIS: We find a better hiding place, that's what we do.
HARD MAN: It's the chance you take.
TOPLIS: The less chances we take the better.
FRENCHMAN [*to* STRANGER]: *Franchement moi je ne voix pas le difficulté. Certains d'entre vous ont des uniformes. Pourquoi pas essayer?*

[*Looks pointedly at* TOPLIS]

Ecoutes. Nous puyons pénétrer dans le camp de détention en deux temps et trois movements et libérer nos camarades.

[*We see* TOPLIS *shaving. He glances at the* STRANGER, *who approaches him*]

STRANGER: He wants us to raid the compound.
TOPLIS: Yes, I gathered. Tell him I might come from Nottingham, but I'm not Robin Hood.
FRENCHMAN: *Moi, je ne comprends rien.*
TOPLIS: We'd be outnumbered a hundred to one, frog-brains.
FRENCHMAN: *Mais nos camarades, ils vont mourir.*
STRANGER: Our comrades will die.

[TOPLIS *is combing his hair in a piece of broken mirror*]

TOPLIS: Yeah, and which of us won't . . .
STRANGER: Jesus, you're a callous bastard, Perce. Doesn't it make you *angry*?
TOPLIS: Don't get angry, get *even*, but we can't get even. Can we? So . . .

65/2. EXT. BRIDGE AND BUILDINGS NEAR BASE BASE CAMP, 9 SEPTEMBER, 1917. DAY

[*An Australian, drunk and standing in front of the Military Police at the bridge, is demanding to be let past into Etaples town.*

We see and re-establish Private HARRY REEVE, *the boxing champion.*

But our focus at first is on a Scots Private and a pretty WAAC he is chatting her up on an incline slightly above the bridge]

SCOTS BOY: I'm from Aberdeen. That's a coincidence, isn't it?
SCOTS WAAC [*blankly and not interested*]: But I'm from Motherwell.
SCOTS BOY: No you know . . . I mean . . . have you been here long?
SCOTS WAAC: Well, I suppose it makes a change from being asked if I come here often.
SCOTS DRUNK: Come on, open the bridge.

REEVE: Come on, you lot, clear off. I'll tell you something for nothing. You're not going anywhere.

[*We move towards the argument on the bridge. The Australian is well backed by fellow Australians and Scots*]

SCOTS DRUNK: Come on. Shut your eyes and we'll swim across.

REEVE: Clear off, otherwise you'll be on charge like your mates.

AUSSIE DRUNK: I'm an officer in disguise. A big officer. A high officer. Let me bloody well through.

REEVE: Only officers. With passes.

AUSSIE DRUNK: I left my pass behind.

REEVE: Go and fetch it then.

AUSSIE DRUNK: I left it behind in Melbourne.

[*Some laughter*]

SCOTS DRUNK: Come on, it's a Sunday afternoon, we've got nothin' to do.

[*More agreement, some jostling, the mood rapidly changing*]

REEVE: There is somethin' you can do – y' can clear off. Now!

AUSSIE DRUNK [*pushing the MP hard*]: I've got four days here, cobber, four days and then who knows – but four days and not another Sunday – and I'm havin' this Sunday in that town.

REEVE: Move back. Move back, now . . . I'm being unusually kind to you, I'm giving you a warning, now –

[REEVE *ducks under the barrier and draws his gun. An MP is tipped over the barrier. The* AUSSIE DRUNK *and assembled men make a rush at the bridge and* REEVE. *He steps a further pace back and fires above their heads. We cut straight to the Scotsman on higher ground. Half his face is gone. He is still leaning back – absurdly. The girl has had her head turned away from him. She hears the firing. Turns to look down, then finally looks towards the Scots boy. The rest start racing at* REEVE, *who is pushed against the side of the bridge. His gun is taken from him.*

As he runs away, we see a group of MPs running towards REEVE *and the soldiers. They see* REEVE *running away. They too turn and run. We see them caught and go down in a flurry of red caps and boots at the far end of the bridge. Man after man spills over them and into the town. Running, cheering, whooping and some of them now armed with pistols*]

66/2. EXT. TOWN SQUARE AND SIDE STREETS DAY

[*We see the hordes as they crash through the town, overturning carts and stalls and people.*

They chase red caps through the alleyways, over walls, a Canary is chased upstairs and dragged out to be pushed downstairs. They smash down the doors of the cafes and estaminets, rolling out barrels of beer and wine into the street and the square.

The rioters also chase MPs through the market stalls. The AUSSIE DRUNK *chases after one MP and points his gun at another who is knocked down against a brazier.*

Two officers, partially dressed, rush out of the brothel.

A Canary is carried to a horse trough and thrown in whilst the horse tethered alongside is released and gallops away]

66A/2. EXT/INT. HOTEL PARIS PLAGE. DAY

[TOPLIS *playing cards in a dining room full of food and silver.]*

TOPLIS [*flatly*]: You lose I think.

[*We see his fellow officers in the hotel room which overlooks the promenade at Paris Plage.*

The losing officer smiles benignly]

67/2. INT. THOMSON'S OFFICE. DAY

[*Quiet comatose shock is written in capital letters all over* THOMSON*'s face. A telephone is in his hand, limply at his side; his uniform has a hurried manner about it.*

GUINNESS *facing him, standing*]

THOMSON: There's nobody here . . . well, hardly anybody here. Of any consequence. Sunday. They're all . . . Paris Plage, having picnics, or hiding behind skirts in the town . . . we should . . . I think we must – have any officers been attacked, Guinness?

GUINNESS: No sir. But that may be because there aren't actually that many –

THOMSON: Yes. *Thank you, Guinness.* Where is Strachan?

GUINNESS: Er picnic sir, Paris Plage.

THOMSON: I want him here and I want runners despatched to Air Base Depots on site, officers to post armed pickets on all gates, all soldiers still in camp turned out and stood to, where they can be seen. And I want the Riot Act and the Army Act relating to mutiny read out to them. Is that understood?

GUINNESS: Sir.

[GUINNESS *turns and leaves*]

68/2. EXT. BASE DEPOT. DAY

[*A* LIEUTENANT COLONEL *on horseback flanked by NCOs is reading the Riot Act to a platoon of soldiers on parade but without rifles.*

The men are restive, cautiously whispering as the news spreads and the background sounds of rioting can be heard.

We see a team of worried gunners nervously guarding their Lewis guns]

LIEUTENANT COLONEL: Every person subject to military law who, on active service, commits any of the aforementioned offences, or endeavours to persuade any person to commit them or, being present, does not use his utmost endeavours to suppress any mutiny or sedition of any of His Majesty's forces shall on conviction by court-martial be liable to suffer death by firing squad. I repeat – shall on conviction by court-martial be liable to suffer death by firing squad.

SOLDIER: Bollocks.

[*The men fidget and, in twos and threes, walk towards and past the Lewis gunners, leaving as the Colonel yells at them to come back. The Lewis gunners desert their machines and join the men*]

69/2. EXT. FORBES CANTEEN. BASE CAMP DAY

[FORBES *and an old French woman in aprons unloading trays of bread and provisions from the back of her car. We hear the approaching rioters: distant shouts of 'into town, lads', 'let's raid the armoury', 'where's the booze' etc.*

Liverpool soldiers come downhill, are joined by Gordon Highlanders and New Zealanders; one of them breaks a window and they stampede into canteen.

FORBES *looks up as her car is surrounded by the men with shouts of 'Angelina – it's Angelina'. They spin her on with them away from her hut towards the town.*

She has no control and is terrified beneath her fixed smile]

FORBES: Is this a revolution?

NEW ZEALANDER: No, ma'am, just a bit of a riot.

[*Laughter and agreement*]

And we're all joining in.

FORBES: Oh well, that's all right then.

[*We see* LADY FORBES *alone trying to compose herself, her clothing and her hair. In an attempt to make a lady-like return. We see two Military Policemen at a doorway to a hut. They run away, followed by the returning soldiers*]

70/2. INT. HOTEL PARIS PLAGE. DAY

OFFICER: Ten.

[TOPLIS *facing a pile of money wins another game and is drawing the money in the centre of the table towards him*]

TOPLIS: Sorry. It's just not your day, eh?

[*He looks at his watch. The officer smiles less benignly than last time*]

71/2. EXT. FORBES CANTEEN/MPS HUT. DAY

[STRACHAN*'s car drives downhill and draws to a halt*]

NEW ZEALANDER: You murdering bastard, Strachan!

[*We see* STRACHAN *in close-up and high blood pressure. He is staring in disbelief at a crowd of rankers enjoying the sight of Sergeants struggling to put out a fire.* STRACHAN *speaks to his WAAC driver*]

STRACHAN: We must get back to your depot immediately, Private Hutchinson.

HUTCHINSON: It's all right, sir.

STRACHAN: Now do as you are told. It is nearly nightfall and no decent woman with any sense would be anywhere near here.

[HUTCHINSON *looks out of her side window as he talks.* STRACHAN *looks in the same direction. We see* LADY FORBES *standing defiant by her still-open refreshment hut, a hut that will remain open for the first thirty-six hours of the mutiny.* HUTCHINSON *and* STRACHAN *exchange glances*]

Precisely my point.

[HUTCHINSON *drives the car off. The soldiers follow, jeering*]

72/2. EXT. THE WAACS' FENCED DEPOT DUSK

[*Protected by some NCOs and officers on the perimeter. A group of men are jeering and making the normal abnormal suggestions.*

HUTCHINSON *is running, under instruction, along with many other WAACs, to the recreation hut to accompanying jeers from the football hooligans amongst the rioters.*

We see through the windows of the recreation hut. As the doors are locked we still hear the chants, noise and ribaldry of the rioters.

A WAAC officer, a stiff-lipped lady of some proportion, tells the WAACs to keep away from the windows]

STIFF LIPS: We shall sing, we shall sing till the *dogs* go home! We shall sing hymns.

[*She starts singing*]

'All things bright and beautiful . . .'

[*Speaks*]

That is an order.

[*Sings*]

'All creatures great and small . . .'

[*WAACs close the windows as they begin to sing. Many are amused and near to giggling. But when a bottle smashes through a window, they grow stronger in voice. One of the WAACs swears at the soldiers.*

'During this time all of us, about five hundred altogether, were locked in the recreation hut with instructions to sing hymns, which we did with our tongues in our cheeks, but with just a little sprinkling of fear in our hearts – the men eventually dispersed, after which we were allowed to stop singing and go to bed.' (*Imperial War Museum: Diary of WAAC Driver*)]

73/2. EXT. TOWN SQUARE. ETAPLES. DUSK

[*Men are drunk everywhere, sprawling and obscene.*

A lorry rattles through the streets. We see a Lewis gun lashed on the back, men huddled behind it. The lorry comes to a halt.

We see that two soldiers are raping two WAACs on the pavement, while a crowd of soldiers encourages them in their actions. We hear a voice from inside the lorry]

VOICE: *Get up, get up!* Get off them – or else!

[*We see the Lewis gun swing down and point in the direction of the crowd. The two men slowly climb off their victims. Four men dismount from the lorry, move towards the grateful sobbing girls, take hold of them and drag them towards the lorry. The* AUSSIE DRUNK, *outside the bakery, sees a Canary making a run for it across the road some thirty yards away*]

AUSSIE DRUNK: Hey, there's another Canary bastard here.

[*A spray of gunfire follows him to the safety of the alleyway, while everyone else dives to the ground*]

74/2. EXT. HOTEL. PARIS PLAGE/PROMENADE INT. FIACRE. NIGHT

[*Outside the hotel.*

We see TOPLIS *in his officer's uniform leaving the hotel. He checks his watch and removes playing cards from his sleeve putting them in a pocket.*

He saunters towards the coast road. 'Shadows shrouding the poplars.' He is followed and casually caught by SECOND LIEUTENANT JAMES DAVIES, *Northumberland Fusiliers*]

DAVIES: I say . . . mind if I walk with you?

TOPLIS [*easily*]: Not at all. Feel free.

DAVIES: I do so like Paris Plage. The sea air. A pleasant meal, good company, forget the horrors . . . for a time.

TOPLIS: . . . Yes.

DAVIES: It's been a remarkable three years . . . for me. Remarkable.

TOPLIS [*wryly, knowing that* DAVIES *wants to talk*]: So you volunteered almost straight away?

DAVIES: First week of the war, August '14, Lieutenant James Davies at your service! Mind you, old boy – came up through the ranks.

Seems like only yesterday I was a private. I was an actor. Before. Treading the boards. In the theatre. The London Palladium.

TOPLIS: Ah.

DAVIES: And you?

TOPLIS: Oh, I er travelled. My parents are in India, you see. In tea. As they say. I was mainly brought up by my aunt and uncle. In York. Because my parents were 'in tea'. For some time as a child I thought they lived in a teapot.

[*Both men laugh.* TOPLIS *grins to himself.* DAVIES *hails a horse-drawn fiacre. Approach the elderly driver.* DAVIES *has the five francs ready*]

DAVIES: Ah, cabbie. Etaples, Monsieur.

[TOPLIS *reaches into his coat pocket, just too late*]

TOPLIS: Please, allow me –

DAVIES: No, no, I insist; I joined you, now you can join me. *Après vous.*

TOPLIS: After you.

DAVIES: *Merci.* How about a couple of stiff ones on the way? That should see us right.

TOPLIS: Ahhh, I have a lady to . . . attend to . . .

DAVIES: Well, one for the road, and the lady, eh? Gather ye rosebuds while ye may . . .

TOPLIS: Absolutely.

DAVIES: After all, 'Life's but a walking shadow. A poor player that struts and frets his hour upon the stage and then is heard no more; it is a tale told by an idiot, full of sound and fury. Signifying nothing.'

[TOPLIS *looks at him flatly*]

Macbeth.

TOPLIS: But of course. Who else . . .

75/2. INT. THOMSON'S OFFICE. NIGHT

[STRACHAN, THOMSON, GUINNESS.
Noise outside increasing rapidly]

STRACHAN: I'm not condoning the buggers, how can I, they ran away, but this isn't a casual street brawl or a case of being improperly dressed –

THOMSON: Get me – I want my office more securely defended to start with – then get GHQ, Guinness.

GUINNESS: Sir.

[GUINNESS *exits*]

THOMSON: But don't sound too windy.

STRACHAN: But it's not small beer, sir, there's thousands of men out there running riot. Mainly with killing and drinking in mind. We have to bring in outside troops.

THOMSON: But . . . if I take them from the front lines there'll be hell to pay . . . though if it doesn't die down, I'm going to have to tell them how serious . . . it's just I'd prefer not to.

[THOMSON *moves to window*]

STRACHAN: That's the least of our worries if this –

THOMSON: *Where have the pickets gone?*

[STRACHAN *looks out of the window as well. We see what the noise has been about: the pickets have indeed gone, to be replaced by men who are piling up a potential bonfire*]

THOMSON: Get me Colonel Nason.

NEW ZEALANDER [O.O.V.]: Clear out, you, we're coming in.

GUINNESS: What on earth do you think you are doing? You can't possibly come in.

[*The door to* THOMSON'*s office opens behind them. We see thrust into the room the officer in charge of the pickets, and some NCOs. We miss a beat, and then several rioters, gas masks and the occasional handkerchief across their faces, enter the room – well armed. Officers and rioters face each other*]

FIRST GAS MASK: Good evening, gentlemen, and welcome to the party . . .

[*The* FIRST GAS MASK *proffers the list of demands to* THOMSON]

76/2. EXT. BASE CAMP. NIGHT

[*Tents burning, men dancing round them. Men jeer at* TOPLIS *and* DAVIES *as they arrive in their carriage.*
Rioters surround the carriage]

RIOTER: Evening, sir.

DAVIES: What's going on? What are they doing?

TOPLIS [*smiling*]: I do believe the worm has turned.

[*Fingering his uniform, he begins to look around. They get out of the fiacre*]

I think I should have arrived more suitably dressed.

DAVIES: Good God almighty! Not a Red Cap in sight!

TOPLIS: Yes, about time too.

DAVIES: Best report to my depot. Come on.

[*Distantly we can hear five hundred WAACs singing 'Silent Night'.* DAVIES *grabs* TOPLIS *and pushes him through the riots to his depot's wooden office in the centre of the blazing bell tents, amid wild hysterical whooping and cheering and baiting. The office is, for the moment, guarded, and we see* TOPLIS *and* DAVIES *forcing themselves into the space near the doorway*]

77/2. INT/EXT. DEPOT OFFICE. NIGHT

[*Inside the office, amid the madness of the noise outside, we see an adjutant alone in a daze*]

DAVIES: Giles, what the hell is going on?

[*A* LIEUTENANT COLONEL *dashes in behind* TOPLIS *and* DAVIES]

LIEUTENANT COLONEL [*to* ADJUTANT]: You sir, take fifty men in battle order, from your depot and take control of number two bridge and the access into town. I said *'you sir!'*

[*The* ADJUTANT *looks at him and is about to get to his feet, when an NCO bursts into the room*]

COMPATRIOT SERGEANT: Sir, sir, permission to speak, sir – some of the bleedin' – the men've surrounded a Red Caps' hut, sir, the whole fu –

[*Tries to compose himself*]

– the whole thing's about to go up – there's brushwood and wooden trestles stacked –

[*The Colonel is already at the door – a door that* TOPLIS *is standing casually by*]

LIEUTENANT COLONEL: All right, all right –

[*Turns back*]

Sir – *take command*!

[*They both rush out into the night.* TOPLIS *leans against the door looking at his watch*]

ADJUTANT [*wearily*]: Davies, take fifty men in battle order from your depot and take control of the number two bridge and the access into town.

DAVIES: Sir!

[DAVIES *and* TOPLIS *exchange a wry glance*]

May I ask, sir, what you intend to be doing, sir? While I'm taking over command.

ADJUTANT [*as the noise increases*]: . . . I'm remaining here to oversee operations.

DAVIES: Sir!

[*He turns towards* TOPLIS *as he speaks*]

Well, Captain, are . . . you willing . . .

[TOPLIS *has gone – the increased noise is due to the door opening. Framed a few yards from the doorway are the threat of soldiers*]

78/2. INT. A BLOCK OF TOILETS. NIGHT

[*The toilets are empty.*

A Gordon Highlander approaches one of the latrines. As he walks down the row, we see him being grabbed head first into the cubicle]

79/2. EXT. BRIDGE NUMBER TWO. NIGHT

[*We see* DAVIES *with his fifty men of the Northumberland Fusiliers with their fixed bayonets and almost fixed expressions.*

They are marching through the rioters, who 'fell back on either side of the column, still booing, jeering and cat-calling, but uncertain about their next move', while searchlights rushed to the scene catch the Royal Fusiliers in their cross-beams.

We see DAVIES *lead his men up the steps of the bridge, and take up position in two ranks across the bridge. And the rioters start to move forward.*

DAVIES, *having lined his men up behind him, turns to face the rioters, looking down upon them, quietly terrified, pistol dangling loose at his side*]

DAVIES [*barely a whisper*]: 'Friends, Romans, Countrymen . . .' No . . .

[*Cheers ring out. The first rioters have reached the bridge.* DAVIES *looks 'casually' behind himself. He sees men with no heart for a fight. Looking away, looking down, looking scared. And someone to the rear of the mob starts playing 'Highland Laddie', the regimental tune of the Gordons, on a bagpipe. The advance continues, many men singing, quietly at first, and then with an edge*]

CHORUS: 'Bonny Willie's gone away, will he no come back again . . .'

[*The piper stops. The singing stops. Even the threats stop. Just the distant sound of 'Onward Christian Soldiers' in soprano. A big burly Highland trooper is inches away from* DAVIES *on the next to top step – so big that he is eyeball to eyeball with* DAVIES. DAVIES *can hear the men at his back coughing nervously, the shuffling of feet*]

DAVIES: Now look, I don't know what the hell has happened here today –

[*The crowd behind the leading Jock seethes forward, shouting*]

FIRST VOICE: Tell him about the murder!

SECOND VOICE: All we want's the bastard police! Just get out of the bloody way!

DAVIES: Yes, all right, and believe me, I share your . . . reservations –

FIRST VOICE: Like shite you do.

SECOND VOICE: And you don't have to suffer them!

[*Cheering*]

DAVIES: – But, *but* this can do no good – and if you all go back to the camp, it can all be sorted out tomorrow. When we've all simmered down.

[*The rioters force and jam themselves further up the steps. Jeering*]

BIG JOCK: Y' can hear them, can't you, sir? It's no' you we're out to get, it's the murderin' Red Caps and the odd Canary we can find, but I must ask you to stand aside. *And if you don't, we'll turn the Lewis guns on you.*

[*Shouts of 'yes' and 'get the guns' greet this.* DAVIES *misses a couple of beats, then turns to face his troops*]

DAVIES: Stand aside, men.

BIG JOCK [*politely*]: Thank you, sir.

[*The Fusiliers are brushed aside rather than standing aside as the rioters storm past them onto and over the bridge. We see* DAVIES, *standing sideways onto the rioters as they race past, staring out, almost blankly.* DAVIES *sees the man with the bagpipe, 'the lemon-squeezer New Zealand hats, the wide-rimmed, side-turned-up Australian headgear, the bottle green glengarries of the Gordon Highlanders –' And as* DAVIES *stands there watching them go, he sees* TOPLIS *dressed as a Private from the Gordon Highlanders going past him, a bundle of clothing under his arm, a gun in his other hand.* TOPLIS *glances at him, smiles and winks. We freeze frame on* TOPLIS]

FADE OUT

EPISODE 3
THE SHAMBLES

79A/3. EXT. TOWN SQUARE. NIGHT

[*Groups of drunken soldiers singing.*

A drunken Bugler making grotesque 'musical' noises. A queue of men outside the officers' brothel.

The door opens and a madame pushes out two dishevelled young men to cheers and jeers from the queue as two of them are allowed in.

At a hotel window overlooking this TOPLIS *looks down on it all.*

One of the brothel queue with a drink in his hand yells up to TOPLIS *who is still wearing his Gordon Highlanders' uniform*]

BROTHEL MAN: Hey. Hey, mate. Come on, mate. Come across. Don't be shy. It's half price tonight.

TOPLIS [*mock embarrassed*]: I'd really like to . . . but I've got this . . . war wound. Enjoy yourselves.

[*The brothel man and his mate look at each other*] BROTHEL MAN: Poor sod.

79B. INT. HOTEL BEDROOM. NIGHT

[TOPLIS *turns from the bedroom window.*

He is wearing only the jacket of the Gordon Highlanders' uniform.

A French girl is asleep in bed]

80/3. INT. THOMSON'S OFFICE. NIGHT

[THOMSON, STRACHAN, *the officer supposedly in charge of the troops who were supposed to be outside, some NCOs.*

The men with the gas masks, guns and handkerchiefs are around the office. Those who are able to are drinking brandy and smoking.

And a piece of paper is in front of THOMSON, *sitting at his desk*]

FIRST GAS MASK [*finally and Australian*]: Just remember this, we're being civilized. Sir. There's men out there who would be inclined otherwise.

SECOND GAS MASK [*flatly, Scottish*]: There's one or two in here as well.

FIRST GAS MASK: So if I were you, I'd just sign that, it's not a lot to ask – it's just asking for some decency. On your part. And that bastard there.

[*Indicates* STRACHAN]

After all, it's only our decency that's keeping you alive.

SECOND GAS MASK: For the time being.

THOMSON: You gave me half an hour.

[*Looks at his watch*]

Forty minutes ago.

FIRST GAS MASK: Christ. I hate heroes.

THOMSON: I will not be threatened and abused in my own office!

[*Points*]

I will not be talked to like this by a Colonial – do you hear me! I will not sign this wretched piece of paper, and I warn you that you will suffer the consequences of your actions.

SECOND GAS MASK: Whoever we are.

[*Some sardonic laughter*]

THOMSON: You are to leave my office. Now. *Now!*

NEW ZEALANDER: Oh, he's getting angry, lads.

[*The* FIRST GAS MASK *rises to confront* THOMSON]

FIRST GAS MASK [*picking up the paper*]: 'The Bull ring to be closed, the Military Police and the Assistant Provost Marshal to be removed.'

[*Looking at* STRACHAN]

That's you, sir – '. . . food and general conditions to be improved, and the town of Etaples to be made more accessible to private soldiers and no reprisals'.

[*Looks up*]

Surely there's nothing wrong with that. Except we spelt 'access-ible' wrong.

THOMSON [*berserk*]: *You have told me what you were going to do – and I have told you. That is all there is to it. I'm not going to do what you want me to do. Are you . . . ?*

[*They look at each other*]

going to do whatever it is you . . . are going to do?

FIRST GAS MASK: Your command of the English language, if I may be so bold, sir, almost rivals your command of this Camp.

SECOND GAS MASK: Well, are we going to do it or what?

FIRST GAS MASK: You won't sign?

THOMSON: Of course I won't.

STRACHAN [*at last*]: 'Gentlemen', your bluff has been called.

[*The* SECOND GAS MASK *cracks* STRACHAN *viciously across the face with the butt of his rifle.* STRACHAN *slumps in his chair but attempts, surprisingly successfully, that air of stoicism of the brave well-bred English gentleman*]

FIRST GAS MASK: Oh well . . .

[*To a* GAS MASK *by the window*]

Is the transport ready?

[*He nods*]

SOLDIER [O.O.V.]: Yes.

SECOND GAS MASK: I'm still for burning the bastards.

FIRST GAS MASK: Not just yet, Jock. This time I think we'll just throw them in the deep end . . . If you would stand, gentlemen, while we escort you to your transport. And no false bravery please, because, believe me, you will need our safe escort just to stay alive.

[*The* SECOND GAS MASK, *who is patently not a nice man, kicks* STRACHAN*'s chair over – with* STRACHAN *in it*]

SECOND GAS MASK: Now get up.

81/82/3. EXT. RIVER BRIDGE. NIGHT

[*We see them come to a stop on the bridge, after the wagon has turned sideways on across the bridge.*

The FIRST GAS MASK *waves the written ultimatum*]

FIRST GAS MASK: Well gentlemen, regretfully we must now part company, until you are ready to agree to our demands.

SECOND GAS MASK: Providin' of course y' can swim.
THOMSON: I have nothing to say.
FIRST GAS MASK: What do you reckon, boys?

[*Much nodding*]

All right, fellers, in they go.

[*The wagon tips up, and slowly slides 'the top echelon of the British Army's No. 1 Base Camp over the parapet and into the river'. However, we see that* THOMSON *has hold of one of the sides of the wagon and refuses to be tipped out. He howls at the rioters*]

THOMSON: My son, my only son, died in the first weeks of the war – he died in battle and you – you bastards, you're still alive.
FIRST GAS MASK: I had three brothers in 1915. Sir. Now I only have one.

[*The* FIRST GAS MASK *slams his revolver butt at* THOMSON*'s fingers until he lets go of the wagon side*]

We've all got hard luck stories – *now get in there!*

[*And we see* THOMSON *join* STRACHAN *and the Durham officer in the river. We watch from the bridge with the gas masks and others as* THOMSON, STRACHAN *and the rest rage away into the shadows of the far river bank. The men begin to take their disguises off and we are reminded again of the relative youth of the soldiers. Many are barely out of their teens*]

Phlegm. Good old British phlegm.
SECOND GAS MASK: No good to y' when y' face is on fire.
FIRST GAS MASK [*shakes his head*]: You can kill as many Red Caps as you can find, Jock, and you'll be all right. Burn down a Brigadier General, mate, you'll be hunted for the rest of your life. No, he has to *give in* . . . and we have to make sure that he does . . . Come on, let's get a drink.

[*As they all turn away from the bridge, we can see the bonfire still smouldering and burning in the near and far distance*]

83/3. INT. HOTEL BEDROOM. NIGHT

[*An Officer's uniform is laid out neatly on a chair.*
TOPLIS *is at the window.*
The town hall clock chimes midnight.
He is still wearing only the jacket of the Gordon Highlanders' uniform.
In the near darkness, we hear a French girl's voice. Broken English]

FRENCH GIRL: *Chéri, chéri* Cruikshank. Come back to bed, yes. I am safe with you in bed.

TOPLIS [*quietly, mocking*]: Safe? I have never been so insulted in my life.

FRENCH GIRL: *Pardon?*

[*He has his gun as he approaches the bed. The girl looks nervously at it*]

TOPLIS: It's all right, I feel safe with *this* in bed.

[*Climbs onto the bed, puts his gun under the pillow and leans close to the girl*]

84/3. INT. THOMSON'S OFFICE. NIGHT

[*A little later that night.*

THOMSON *is wet through from his considerable stomach downwards. He doesn't care. He is going ape shit – on the telephone. A battered* GUINNESS *and the* CORPORAL CLERK *in attendance*]

THOMSON: I don't want the Cavalry Corp HQ, so it doesn't matter if there's no one there, does it – I want the 9th Cavalry Brigade, Good God, man, of course there's a bloody difference . . . I want the Corps Commander, shall I spell it?

[*He puts the telephone down, then picks it up again, having to crank it to get through. We hear the dull thud of a distant explosion*]

Will you also continue to telephone GHQ, and do not be put off by some pimply little corporal. Thank you.

[*Looks up towards his own pimply little* CORPORAL CLERK]

Where was I?

CORPORAL CLERK [*reading notes*]: – 'Feeling in the crowd was only against the Police and Officers were treated respectfully . . .'

THOMSON: Yes. 'However the demeanour of the crowd was so threatening towards the police, that they were obliged to retreat. The officers gradually got the men back to camp and by twenty-two hundred hours – 22.30, all was quiet.'

[*And we hear a raucous group of men running, singing and cheering past.* THOMSON *sits blankly facing out. The* CORPORAL CLERK *cannot help but look at a clock that indicates ten to one*]

They took all the . . . drink?

[GUINNESS *nods.* THOMSON *looks at* GUINNESS*'s bruised face*]

They did that to you?

[GUINNESS *nods again*]

I'm sorry.

[*Looks away quickly*]

86/3. EXT. TOWN SQUARE. DAY

[*We see* ASSER *and* THOMSON *drive up in* THOMSON*'s car, well guarded. They are in the centre of the town; it is still very early morning.*

There are clear remnants of the night before: men are lying down, dead drunk. Fires are still smouldering, knots of rioters are at street corners and down alleyways leading off the square, sullen, armed and watching]

ASSER: They must have risen very early this morning, General.

[THOMSON *looks at* ASSER *and then around*]

THOMSON: Who . . . must?

ASSER [*waving his arm*]: All the men whom you assured me were back in the camp by ten o'clock last evening . . . Perhaps they have a problem with regard to sleepwalking.

THOMSON: My information was . . .

[*Almost in a frightened whisper*]

Look, the situation is still almost under control but of course it could get worse, and –

ASSER: I don't think it will.

THOMSON: What?

ASSER: Yes, I know – the Bolsheviks, the French Mutiny in the summer, socialists and strikes in our green and pleasant land. But I think this is different.

[*Faces* THOMSON]

This is not, I suspect, political – more . . . personal.

[*Then turns away*]

I suggest you get the remaining men back down to the Bull-ring . . .

THOMSON [*Flatly*]: Training Camp Number One.

ASSER: Yes, well get them down there with the . . . 'instructors', make sure the officers and NCOs keep a reasonably pleasant but tight grip on what's left of the base, and we'll see what tonight brings.

THOMSON: What if it brings . . .

ASSER: GHQ will have to consider bringing reinforcements from the front.

THOMSON [*uneasily*]: I have kept this situation at a deliberately rather low . . . level of priority with Headquarters. I thought if I could whistle up the Cavalry, the matter could be –

ASSER: Hushed up?

THOMSON: Cleared up. Very quickly.

[TOPLIS *comes out of a hotel and moves off down the road*]

ASSER: By the way, have you seen Strachan at all?

THOMSON: Not since last night, no.

ASSER: He hasn't disappeared too, has he?

THOMSON: Not that I am aware, and I doubt it very much, knowing Strachan.

ASSER: Good. Good. Still, if he has, you can always start dragging the river for him . . . Can't you?

[*The car moves off to jeers*]

88/3. EXT. SANCTUARY WOODS. CAVES. DAY

[*We see the sanctuary, a new one, perhaps a series of shelters, more loose in situation than before, and now more loose in atmosphere as well.*

We see the collected gas masks and handkerchiefs from the previous night.

The socialist STRANGE *and the few politically minded deserters are present.*

TOPLIS *is at the slightest of distances from them and so is* HARD MAN.

In the background are as many men as possible, lounging about, laughing, soaking in the news from Etaples.

Some have soaked it in the night before and are now regretting it]

FIRST GAS MASK: – Yeah all right – we're out to make some trouble. That's about it really, isn't it?

[*The other gas masks nod*]

We thought you might be able to give us a hand.

STRANGE: Why's that?

FIRST GAS MASK: Oh you know, the rumours we hear about you boys – agitators, revolutionaries.

SECOND GAS MASK: I don't see any red flags.

STRANGE: As far as I know, there are two Bolsheviks here, four men on the run from the aftermath of the French Mutiny, and one or two part-time socialists. The others are –

TOPLIS: Don't forget the pacifist.

FIRST GAS MASK [*easily*]: Okay, forget politics, how about revenge? A lot of your lads are still stuck in the prison compound, waiting around for a death sentence.

SECOND GAS MASK: The place can be ours, lock, stock and gun barrel.

TOPLIS: Until when?

FIRST GAS MASK: Does it matter – we're due for the Front in less than a week.

HARD MAN: I'm not.

[*Silence*]

FIRST GAS MASK: Look, we can win, you know. We can beat them for ourselves, and get better conditions for the men who . . . come after us.

TOPLIS: Sounds very political to me.

[*Grins at them*]

FIRST GAS MASK: Hiding away here isn't going to do anything, is it?

STRANGE: I agree with you, but I can't force anyone . . .

SECOND GAS MASK: Suit yourself, we only came for a walk anyway.

[*To* FIRST GAS MASK]

So much for those stories about hundreds of desperate, passionate, violent men.

[*Laughs at them*]

Two Bolsheviks, four froggie deserters, one union socialist, a pacifist, a few drunks and a lot of –

HARD MAN: I'd be careful what you say next, mate.

FIRST SHADOW: We can get ten times this number here within an hour.

SECOND GAS MASK: And what will you do – sing songs around the camp fire? Where's Baden Powell? Or would you lot prefer his sister?

STRANGE: Percy, you talk to the lads.

FIRST GAS MASK: Ah come on, will y', Tommy.

STRANGE: Listen, Perce, I can't make public speeches. I would if I could but I can't. I know what to say but I can't make people follow me that way.

[*Silence.* STRANGE *looks to* TOPLIS]

TOPLIS: Yeah, well someone better had 'cos these lads are right. They're all going up the line in a couple of days and you know as well as I do they'll be no worse off at the Front than at the bloody camp. Bugger it. Those bastards in Etaples started this. Their sort always do. Well, this time let's see if we can't finish it. Give us an hour!

FIRST GAS MASK: Right. Great. See you at the bridge.

TOPLIS [*to* STRANGE]: And you'd better give me some big words.

[*Looks away*]

I don't know what's got into me today, I feel really kind of . . . 'honourable'. *But it won't last.*

89/3. EXT. FARMHOUSE. DAY

[*We see a large house, on the roadway between Paris Plage and Etaples.*

It is washing day. A red skirt is on a washing line with other things.

We see, moving across our screen and past the house, obscuring both house and washing line, some of the deserters.

One takes the skirt off the line and returns to the group]

90/3. EXT. BRIDGE. DAY

[*We see them arriving at the River Canche bridge.*

Several men sporting very make-shift red flags – and new philosophies.

We see the men at the head of the mob: TOPLIS, *the* STRANGER, *the* HARD MAN, *the* GAS MASKS]

FIRST GAS MASK: What next?

TOPLIS: How well do you know this camp?

FIRST GAS MASK: We've only been here ten days . . .

[*Shrugs*]

But we'll never forget it.

TOPLIS: All right, if we want to cause as much trouble as possible, we split the men up –

[*Looks at the mob*]

– four groups – four times the trouble – four different places.

SECOND GAS MASK [*sardonically*]: Should have been a bleedin' officer.

TOPLIS [*grins*]: I know, you're not the first to remark upon it.

[*Turns to* STRANGE]

We'll take the detention compound.

[*To the* HARD MAN]

Franny, go down the Bullring, see what you can do there, for memory's sake.

[*To the* GAS MASKS]

One of you can go down and get the rest of your fellows together, smash the trains, anything.

SECOND GAS MASK: And what happens then?

TOPLIS: If I knew that I'd be reading palms. But if we just sit on our arses they won't sign anything. If they don't come to us, we'll go to them.

[*As the men start to split up and reassemble, we see* STRANGE *at* TOPLIS*'s side, looking at him*]

STRANGE: You really love this, don't you?

TOPLIS: *Yeah.* And you know why, Strange? 'Cos it's all bollocks . . . *and I don't care.*

STRANGE: Oh yes you do.

91/3. INT. STRACHAN'S QUARTERS. DAY

[STRACHAN*'s face is showing signs of the battering he received earlier. He is sitting drinking and drinking – quietly.*

THOMSON, *in full uniform and bandaged fingers, is facing him*]

STRACHAN: We'll not go yet, Andrew, not yet, that's not the Army way. It will be all brushed under the carpet, shovelled out of sight, seemingly forgotten about and then one fine day six months from now, we'll both be posted to the Outer Hebrides, in preparation for a campaign against Iceland.

THOMSON: All I'm concerned about –

STRACHAN: And they will call it 'promotion'.

THOMSON: Where are your men – apart from outside here guarding you?

STRACHAN: Some are inside.

[*Looks towards a door*]

A second line of defence in the servants' quarters . . . Otherwise, I don't know. Probably forming their own 'sanctuaries' in the forests. Now that would be ironic.

THOMSON: If we have another night like last night, I'll just have to . . . to make the situation more . . . defined. I thought I would get the Cavalry like that –

[*Flicks his fingers*]

– swords and horses, mounted steel, soon sort them out – but . . . old friends, I had old friends in the Cavalry – Dickie Charlesworth . . . Freddie Hawkins. They are all in meetings or on leave, so I'm told . . .

[GUINNESS *comes through the door leading to the hall. He presents* THOMSON *with two messages.* THOMSON *speeds through them*]

Reinforcements for the Front are piled up at Boulogne awaiting the restoration of discipline and order. Every single man we sent down to Camp One for training has sat on the sand and refused to budge.

[*Glances up*]

A mere three and a half thousand men. Guinness, tell my driver I'll be down in one minute.

GUINNESS: Sir.

STRACHAN: Andrew, I'd be glad to offer a few of my men as an armed escort but it might be rather pointless.

THOMSON: Yes.

92/3. EXT. DETENTION COMPOUND. DAY

[*We see the prisoners' detention compound.*
TOPLIS *at the head of a large group of deserters and rioters.*
There is jeering and shouting.
They are well armed, one way or another.
A few 'red flags' are in evidence.
We see the prison guards inside the fence.
TOPLIS *is talking to a Welsh NCO guard*]

TOPLIS: I'm offering to save your life.

WELSH NCO GUARD: That's very generous of you, I'll remember you for that.

TOPLIS: You may not have the chance to. Look. The choice is yours – open up and clear off – or stay and get beaten to buggery.

[*Pause. The* NCO GUARD, *whispers, with little lip movement*]

WELSH NCO GUARD: Do us a favour, no guns.

[TOPLIS *looks at him*]

We won't use our guns if you don't use yours.

TOPLIS: We weren't planning to.

WELSH NCO GUARD: You know, you see, we've got to put up a . . .

show. There might be . . . informers. So, er, sort of, like keep the prisoners away from us for Christ's sake, and we have a quick tussle and a bit of bruising . . . What do you say?

TOPLIS: Fine by me.

[TOPLIS *indicates for him to come nearer. Then pistol whips him across the face, viciously*]

Will that be all right?

[*We see the rioters and mutineers flourish into the compound, with little resistance shown by the rest of the guards – to the barely hidden disappointment on the rioters' behalf. We see the shaven heads of the men being released. We see, particularly, the small Bantam Corporal,* GILZEAN, *and the* GEORDIE *– who is extremely happy. The* GEORDIE *approaches* TOPLIS, *greeting and hugging him*]

GEORDIE: Percy, Percy! I knew it, I soddin' well knew it. I said you'd get me out of here, I told them. And you bloody well have, the lot of us too. You're a hero, Perce, a flamin' hero, man!

[*The* GEORDIE *and the others run towards the guards, and it is they who supply the edge to the violence*]

TOPLIS [*watching him go*]: And you're one boring bastard.

93/3. EXT. ROAD TO DETENTION COMPOUND DAY

[*We see* THOMSON *in his open car, alone apart from his driver. He sees a smouldering burnt-down building. There are a few men about. The car stops*]

THOMSON: . . . What was that?

THOMSON'S DRIVER: It was the picture house, sir.

THOMSON: How stupid. Their recreation facilities. Gone.

THOMSON'S DRIVER: Yes sir. It was Charlie Chaplin sir, very popular with the men, sir.

THOMSON: Seemingly. A comedian, I understand.

[*And along the road towards them come marching, flag waving, shouting and singing,* TOPLIS *and the large group, all having joined together again, gas masks and handkerchiefs galore, but not on* TOPLIS]

Wait, wait. I'm going to speak to these men.

[*We see* THOMSON *standing up in his open-backed car as the rebels, prisoners and deserters approach – and then surround him*]

Get back to your units. Report back to your depots. Every man of you.

RIOTER: It's that bastard Thomson.

FIRST GAS MASK: Put your masks on. Masks on.

THOMSON: Call yourselves soldiers, *British* soldiers, soldiers of the –

[*We can hear no more. A mass of men scrummage around the car, trying to turn it over, amidst such shouts as 'go and have another swim' and 'quick, it's high tide' – subtle stuff like that. The* FIRST GAS MASK, *the socialist* STRANGE *and* GILZEAN *manage to form a cordon around* THOMSON *and prevent him from being manhandled. He 'sits' down in his car as all the bouncing occurs. As everything settles,* TOPLIS *jumps onto the running board, and then into the car. He sits by* THOMSON *– who stares ahead.* TOPLIS *makes himself at home. He reaches out of the car, takes the manifesto off the* FIRST GAS MASK *and present it to* THOMSON]

TOPLIS: Our demands. You've seen them before, I believe.

THOMSON: Get out of my car.

TOPLIS: Oh come on, don't be like that –

THOMSON: Get out of my car.

TOPLIS: But I've always believed that whatever's mine is yours, and whatever's yours is mine. Mainly because you've got more than me.

THOMSON: Get out of my car.

TOPLIS [*mimicking perfectly*]: 'Get out of my car.'

[*Laughter*]

THOMSON: The Cavalry will be here by nightfall.

[*Finally looks properly at* TOPLIS]

By nightfall. Do you understand that? You will soon be cut down to size then. Is that your uniform, private?

TOPLIS: For the time being, yes. But if we can –

THOMSON: But you're not a Highlander, you're not even a Scot.

TOPLIS: No, you see, I was on holiday in Edinburgh when war broke out –

[TOPLIS *holds the paper up to* THOMSON]

THOMSON: Get out of my car.

TOPLIS: Agree to our demands.

THOMSON: }
TOPLIS: } [*together*] Get out of my car.

TOPLIS: [*flatly, as he gets out of car*]: We're going to win. We are, you know.

THOMSON: You'll regret this.
TOPLIS: Not as much as you will. Sir.
[THOMSON *stares out. The rioters hesitate*]
THOMSON: Drive on. *Drive on.*
[*The car moves on. The men swear and spit and jeer and push out. But the car drives through them – and the leaders look to* TOPLIS]
FIRST GAS MASK: Cavalry?
GEORDIE: Christ.
TOPLIS: So he says.
GILZEAN: The Cavalry's done nothin' in this war, they'd delight in doing the likes of us.
TOPLIS: Well, you heard what the man said. Nightfall. We have till nightfall. Let's see what happens at 'nightfall'.
[*Grins*]
Until then, we may as well make the most of it. I mean, be a shame to waste the opportunity.

94/3. INT. THOMSON'S OFFICE. DAY

[THOMSON *back in his office, on the telephone. He throws the telephone down.*
GUINNESS *knocks and enters*]

GUINNESS: The Chief Provost Marshal and General Asser, sir.
[THOMSON *stands*]
THOMSON: Good afternoon, gentlemen.
[BRIGADIER GENERAL HORWOOD, *Chief Provost Marshal of the Armies and* ASSER *enter*]
HORWOOD: Afternoon. A bad business, Andrew. Gone too far now . . . no choice. Outside troops.
THOMSON: It looks like it.
ASSER: Withdrawn from the Front.
[*Silence*]
HORWOOD: Well, how many?
ASSER: And for how long?
THOMSON: Depends on who they are. I thought the Cavalry, decent men . . . Regular Soldiers . . .
HORWOOD: You'll get the best we can give you.
ASSER: You know the situation, Andrew. The big push is on.
THOMSON: Yes, thank you. How quickly can the men be got here?

HORWOOD: Possibly by . . . tomorrow night. Possibly. Till then you'll just have to do the best you can. You know where you can find us.

[*They are about to turn and leave. The telephone rings on* THOMSON*'s desk. He hesitates slightly.* ASSER *and* HORWOOD *watch him*]

THOMSON: Excuse me. Hello – Yes . . . Ah.

[*Sudden sweetness and shite*]

Yes . . .

[*Looks up*]

Could you ask . . . him to hold on, please. Just a few moments . . . Thank you.

[*Puts the telephone down.* ASSER *and* HORWOOD *wait, looking enquiringly at* THOMSON. *He tries to smile, partly in an attempt at dismissal. Then moves with them towards the doorway*]

Thank you, General – General Asser, thank you.

[*Both men nod formally, exchange curious glances.* THOMSON *opens the door*]

HORWOOD: Oh and by the way, Andrew, you ought to know . . . Strachan's gone.

THOMSON: . . . Gone? But I was with him . . .

HORWOOD: Yes, transferred at his own request. About an hour ago – very sensible . . . all things considered – he sends his regards.

ASSER [*flatly*]: No doubt you'll see him again.

THOMSON: Yes. No doubt.

[ASSER *and* HORWOOD *go.* THOMSON *hastens to his desk, and telephone*]

Hello . . . operator . . . *Oper* – ah hello . . . I was speaking to Brigadier Charlesworth . . . yes . . . Dickie, *Dickie!* My God, it's a pleasure to hear your voice . . . yes, a long time, a very long time . . . Listen Dickie, there's a spot, well a lot of trouble here. I've been trying to contact you since Sunday night, we . . . I see, you know about the events . . . Listen, I'll come straight to the point, I need some assistance and as soon as possible, I need your men; horses and swords, *put the fear of God up the buggers*.

[GUINNESS *enters and waits at the desk to hand* THOMSON *a piece of paper*]

I need . . .

[*Sighs*]

. . . Oh three hundred men, *that's all*, but it will all be taken out of my hands if you don't – if things don't improve . . . if you could tell me by . . . tomorrow morning, if you can do that, if that's possible . . . what? . . . Oh yes, Kipling. 'If'. Yes, yes, 'if you can keep your head when all about you' . . . No doubt appropriate, but I'm not in the mood for poetry, Dickie . . . yes, all right, thank you for telephoning.

[THOMSON *has moved about during the telephone call, to the window, etc. Where he has seen glimpses and remnants of anarchy. And he has gone through almost all the emotions as he talked. When he puts the telephone down, he breathes out deeply, sits at his desk and his whole body seems to deflate*]

95/3. INT. FORBES' CANTEEN. DAY

[*We see* LADY FORBES *in her tea hut, at the counter assisted by another lady who is in the background frying eggs furiously.*

Bread, cakes, cases of eggs, cigarettes, large urns of tea, etc. abound.

A queue of men are ordering.

We see GENERAL ASSER *enter from the rear of the hut. Two armed guards are with him. He quietly watches, as the men shout their orders*]

SECOND GAS MASK: Three egg sandwiches, miss, and a couple of Woodbines.

FIRST SHADOW: Three teas please, Angelina.

SECOND GAS MASK: Oh, and one General on toast please.

[*Laughter as* LADY FORBES *turns around to see* ASSER. ASSER *ignores the jibe, but he is obviously very ill at ease. He approaches* LADY FORBES]

ASSER: Can I speak to you, Angela?

FORBES: I'm far too busy at the moment.

[*As she supplies the three teas*]

ASSER: I really must insist. Could you –

[FORBES *turns to him, wiping her hands on her apron. Puzzled, she leaves her counter and moves to him*]

FORBES: Well? Whatever is the matter?

ASSER: I'm accompanying Brigadier Horwood.

FORBES: Well, not a pleasant experience, I'll admit, but not one to merit quite this much gloom, surely.

ASSER: I have a message from him.

FORBES [*jokingly*]: To order me out of the camp.

ASSER: Almost correct. You are to leave France.

FORBES [*she laughs*]: Don't talk such rot, Johnnie.
ASSER: It's an order.
FORBES: But why?
ASSER: Strachan's gone.
FORBES: Good, I'm very glad to hear it. So?
ASSER: So you have to go too.
FORBES: But I don't understand.
ASSER: It's all to do with enemies . . .
FORBES: And I thought our enemy was Germany.
ASSER: There's a car waiting for you to take you back to your house.
FORBES: To pack?
ASSER: Yes. I'm sorry, Angela. I'll come with you.
FORBES [*near to tears*]: Is that an order too?
ASSER: Yes. I suppose it is. Come on, let's get it over with.
FORBES: Can't I even . . . Goodbye?
ASSER: No.
FORBES: But I don't understand. I didn't do anything wrong.
ASSER: . . . There are always casualties . . . innocent victims.
FORBES [*takes off her apron*]: Yes, but I've been stabbed in the back, haven't I?

[*She throws down the apron and walks towards the door leading out of the building*]

96/3. INT. ETAPLES. HOTEL BAR. NIGHT

[TOPLIS, STRANGE, *sitting at a table.*

Around them are some of the others already established. The HARD MAN, *the prime* GAS MASKS, *the* GEORDIE, FRENCHIE *etc.*]

TOPLIS: 'Nightfall'.
STRANGE: And no sign.
FIRST GAS MASK: They won't arrive now.
TOPLIS: Not tonight, no.

[*Looks around*]

But they'll come. Machine guns, horses or swords, whatever, they'll come. They have to.
SECOND GAS MASK: Let the bastards come.
STRANGE: . . . Yes, and we'll probably see our own brothers turning on us.
TOPLIS: 'Course they will. They'll beat seven shades of shite out of

anyone they can get hold of. And if their officers say, 'Shoot the sods,' then they'll do it, because it'll be us or them. No, we've only got one chance. If we can get Thomson to give in, the demands become officially recognized –

[*Glances at* STRANGE]

– good hey? – 'officially recognized' – if they do, then it might be hard for the top brass to go back on the word of an officer.

FIRST GAS MASK: And a gentleman.

TOPLIS: Oh aye yeah, that an' all.

[*Mimics to laughter*]

'Get out of my car . . .'

FIRST GAS MASK: Anyway there's not much we can do tonight.

TOPLIS: Oh I don't know, you can enjoy yourselves.

[*The small Corporal enters as* TOPLIS *finishes. Very flushed*]

GILZEAN: Hey lads, there's two Red Caps and a Canary been spotted in a garret on the Rue de Montpelier. Come on.

[*The others depart enthusiastically, leaving* TOPLIS *and* STRANGE]

STRANGE: You're not . . . joining in?

TOPLIS [*officer-like as he lights a cigar*]: Oh no, I don't think so – I do so find killing people terribly . . . boring. Shall we do something else, Charles?

[TOPLIS *stands, motions* STRANGE *to follow him. He takes a bunch of roses from the bar and they go upstairs*]

97/3. INT. ETAPLES HOTEL. CORRIDOR. NIGHT

STRANGE: . . . How . . . where did you learn . . . ?

[*Waves his hands ineffectually*]

TOPLIS: Yes, Charles?

STRANGE: Oh I don't know . . . how old are you?

TOPLIS: . . . Twenty. Very recently, in fact. And not a card, nor a kiss or a handshake.

STRANGE: But what happened to you to make you like this?

TOPLIS: . . . Nothing. 'Nothing' worthwhile . . . happened to me. And nothing was ever going to. So I decided to do something about it.

STRANGE: When was that?

TOPLIS: Oh, I think I was about seven at the time.

[*They reach* TOPLIS*'s room at the inn.* TOPLIS *stands at the door. There is another bedroom door close by*]

STRANGE: You'll be, er, seeing that girl now. I'll –
[*Motions off*]

TOPLIS: Yes I will, but I thought you might like to keep us . . . sort of company. In a sort of fashion.

STRANGE: Me? *Company*? Oh no. God, no. I couldn't do that.

TOPLIS: No, Charles, I didn't mean *that*. No. I'm not in the habit of sharing. It's more like, you know, you see somebody like me with a pretty girl, like you did yesterday, and of course, you always say, 'She hasn't got a sister by any chance, has she?' Well . . .
[TOPLIS *leans across and knocks on the door next to his, then opens it.* STRANGE *stares in, then closes the door and looks for the stairs – for a second. Then points at the closed door. Then at* TOPLIS*'s door. His stammer and his face become briefly vivid*]

STRANGE: . . . Her sister? That's her sister?
[TOPLIS *knocks on the door again*]

TOPLIS: A sort of sister, Charles. Shall we say, a sister of mercy.
[TOPLIS *opens the door for* STRANGE. *Then gently pushes him into the room*]

97A. INT. HOTEL BEDROOM. NIGHT

[*The French girl is lying on the bed reading a magazine.*
There is a knock on the door.
She gets up, opens the door and TOPLIS *enters, his hand behind his back. He reveals the bunch of flowers*]

FRENCH GIRL: *Tu es revenu, et des fleurs.*
[*She puts her arms round him*]

98/3. INT. THOMSON'S OFFICE. NIGHT

[THOMSON *drinking. Heavily. Facing out*]

THOMSON: Come here . . . Guinness . . . here. *No, here.* Get yourself a drink. Sit.
[*As* THOMSON *motions to a seat near him, we see* GUINNESS. *He finally sits down. He too faces out. Most of the time*]

That's it . . . Drink.

[THOMSON *pours him a drink.* THOMSON *pours himself another one*]

Don't mind if I do . . . Well . . . it's all bollocks, isn't it? Guinness.

[*No answer*]

That's what the men would say, isn't it? 'All bollocks'. Rankers' language. There's an officers' expression, officers' language if you wish – 'You're going to get a bowler hat' . . . Means someone's going to be sent home. Sacked. Sent somewhere out of the way. 'The Outer Hebrides'. . . . did you know, Guinness, that I was a Commandant of the Royal Military Academy at Woolwich? A coveted appointment. September 1908. I was . . . those young officer cadets, they looked up at me, I had a way with them. *Yes*, I was respected, Guinness . . . I may well have been held in some affection . . . Remember that long hot summer of 1911? Day after day after glorious day . . . and one day I announced that parades could be held in shirt sleeves. I thought it was an act of generosity. But I made enemies that day. I know I did. I know now too that I made enemies when I sponsored end-of-term dances, when I encouraged the Academy's dramatic society.

[*Glances at* GUINNESS]

My wife was a keen amateur actress, lovely soprano . . . but knives were being sharpened.

[*Drinks and pours again*]

And at the end of that summer, that long hot summer of 1911, the Chief of the Imperial General Staff, Sir John French, yes, Sir John French, came down for our open day. You know the usual sort of thing, Guinness . . . well, perhaps you don't . . . usually full of platitudes and congratulations and back slapping, breast beating about patriotism and loyalty . . .

[*Drinks, pours, drinks again. Tears welling in his eyes*]

. . . Not that summer of . . . oh no, no indeed. I stood beside Sir John French, facing my cadets, their parents and friends, members of my own family, *while he attacked me for the lack of discipline at Woolwich.*

[*He is now crying very quietly*]

Had to take it like a man while he demanded a return to . . . proper standards of dress . . . more drill, less leave . . . and an end to our 'hectic' social life. That's what he said. I stood by his side, eyes facing front, and that's what he said. I left Woolwich shortly after.

[*Long pause. We perhaps see a look of ill-disguised contempt on* GUINNESS*'s face. We see the tears tearing down* THOMSON*'s face*]

. . . And I returned to King's Regulations, to the very letter of the law . . .

[*Stands up, moves towards the door with his drink*]

. . . no more small indulgences . . . the bastards could parade in Hell without a shirt sleeve to be seen, for all I cared.

[*Goes out of the door. Looks back at* GUINNESS. *Closes the door.* GUINNESS *is left in the room. Promptly reaches for the whisky bottle*]

GUINNESS: . . . Gone and never called me 'mother'.

99/3. EXT/INT. SCOTTISH IBD. DAY

[*We see* GILZEAN, TOPLIS *and* STRANGE *approaching the hut.*]

GILZEAN: . . . So what kind of night did you have anyway?

TOPLIS: Oh quiet really, Gilzean, we were both merely wrapped in the arms of the two most beautiful women in France.

GILZEAN: Oh I know, the Mata Hari was at me all night long, wouldn't take 'no' for an answer . . .

[*We hear a flourish of garbled arguments for and against an end to the mutiny, even a sprinkling of French and Russian.*

Some sort of silence arrives with TOPLIS, STRANGE *and* GILZEAN]

VOICE: We should stop now.

SECOND GAS MASK: If we do we've lost everything and you bet your lives them bastards'll give us a right hammering.

FIRST SHADOW: I agree. I've got me own fight with the English and I'm not giving in now. Up the Republic. Afterwards.

HARD MAN: Why don't we raid Thomson's office and take him hostage, or better still the WAACs.

VOICE: Yes, let's take the WAACs hostage. They're still down there singing their heads off.

FIRST GAS MASK: Morning, gentlemen. Sit down.

[*Space is made for* GILZEAN, TOPLIS *and* STRANGE]

Well friends, it seems we can't do much more. We can go on running wild, we can go on making demands, but sooner or later –

GEORDIE: Sooner than you think!
FIRST GAS MASK [*shrugs*]: Soon enough, they'll bring in a Division, they'll bring in a new detachment of military police.
VOICE: What about the Cavalry?
FIRST GAS MASK: The only argument is about when we stop, how we stop . . .
[*Looks at* TOPLIS]
TOPLIS: *If we stop.*
SECOND GAS MASK: It's all right for you deserters.
[*The group argues about continuing the fight, voices raised*]
STRANGE: If I can just say, I want to stay here as long as I can. I came here as a socialist to support my brothers.
TOPLIS: Not to mention sisters. All right, all right, if you really want to know, I think you've got one last big bluff. But you've got to do it now. Listen . . .
[*We fade*]

100/3. EXT. AMMUNITION DUMP. DAY

[*We see the area around the ammunition dump.*
Some of the rioters are moving Lewis guns into place, gas masks and handkerchiefs in position.
A leading GAS MASK presents a letter to the officer in charge, with some formality. We see the letter being taken very seriously.]

101/3. EXT/INT. THOMSON'S OUTER OFFICE

[THOMSON, GUINNESS, *the* CORPORAL CLERK. *Plus a messenger from the ammunition dump.*
THOMSON *is reading the note. A clock indicates five to three*]

THOMSON: Get my car, I want my car.
[*The telephone rings as* THOMSON *re-reads the demand. He stops reading.* GUINNESS *answers the telephone, listens, puts the receiver down.* THOMSON *waits*]
GUINNESS: Thank you. Major Dugdale, sir, the pickets have given way on Number One Bridge again.
[*Looks down at his notes*]

'Too many men to count – [*He looks up*] have gone through.' Sir.

THOMSON: . . . Get me my car.

GUINNESS: Your car is outside, sir.

[THOMSON *leaves. We can see him approach and get into his car. As* THOMSON *does so, the telephone rings again on* GUINNESS*'s desk.* GUINNESS *answers it and listens, makes notes*]

Yes. 19th Hussars. Yes, sir. I'm afraid . . . he's left the office, sir.

[*Looks out. Sees* THOMSON *in his car, still stationary*]

. . . I'm terribly sorry, Brigadier Charlesworth, I don't know where he's gone . . . and it'll be too late to catch him now, sir, but I'll make sure he receives your message as soon as he returns . . . Thank you, sir . . .

[*He puts the telephone down as* THOMSON*'s car moves off, and meets the puzzled look of the* CORPORAL CLERK. GUINNESS *puts his head down and begins to write*]

102/3. INT/EXT. THE MUTINY HEADQUARTERS IN THE SCOTS IBD. DAY

[*Crowded, silent, cigarette smoke lying heavy in the air.* GILZEAN *is at the window looking out, suddenly taking a fresh interest*]

GILZEAN: *Thomson*!

[*Many of the men move urgently towards the windows to watch.* TOPLIS *goes to look out of the back window and the back door. We see, from the POV of the men in the hut, as* THOMSON *arrives and a mob of men outside surround the car. We hear the shouts and jeers, see some attempts to bounce the car and* THOMSON. *We see him stand up and appear to begin his 'call yourselves soldiers' routine*]

THOMSON: Listen. Listen to me. After some consideration I am prepared to make some compromises and I am prepared to accede to some of your demands.

[*The men at the front who have surrounded him are again deliberately protecting him, and they shout the rest of the men down. Something resembling order is restored. Then we see* THOMSON, *standing head down, talking to his boots. Ripples of excitement, followed by sudden uproar spreading from those nearest to* THOM-

SON. *Hats go in the air, but not aimed at* THOMSON. *Joy is in the air. Poor girl. We see the* GEORDIE *and the* HARD MAN *and a couple of the lesser* GAS MASKS *forcing their way through the crowd around* THOMSON. *They burst in, the* GEORDIE *exultant*]

GEORDIE: He's come to sign the demands!

SECOND GAS MASK: Strachan's away, the police aren't coming back –

HARD MAN: The Bullring's closed!

GEORDIE: Better pay and conditions –

SECOND GAS MASK: And the town's open to everyone!

GEORDIE: The lot, I'm tellin' y', the bloody lot!

[*There is a mixture of quiet relief and an elated sense of victory and achievement amongst the men. Some shake hands and hug each other*]

GILZEAN: He's coming in here.

[STRANGE *and the others return to the table and the written demand.* TOPLIS *sees* THOMSON *struggling determinedly towards the hut. We can also see him through the open doorway, still some yards away*]

TOPLIS [*loudly*]: What are you doing? Hide your faces, hide them, turn them away, f' Christ's sake!

[*They stare at him*]

This isn't the bloody end of it – not if he sees you, you idiots.

[*Some movement*]

Unless you want to come with us, hide your faces.

[*We see men putting gas masks back on furiously, handkerchiefs around their faces. One or two just face the wall. One man opens a cupboard and finds a tank driver's chain-mail mask, used to protect driver's faces against splinters. He looks almost medieval and scaring in appearance.* STRANGE, *however, makes no attempt to hide his face*]

TOPLIS: Cover your face, Strange, cover it.

STRANGE: Why – I've done noth –

TOPLIS: Because, you stupid bastard, you're going to be somebody after this war – you want to be somebody – what do you want to be known as – if you get that far – a socialist or a deserter?

[*Looks behind himself to the door*]

Don't argue the toss – just do it!

[STRANGE *reluctantly puts his hand over his face.* TOPLIS *grabs a handkerchief out of his pocket, holds it to his face.* THOMSON *enters, to see the bizarre appearance of the men in the hut. He sees the men ranged around the table, the written demand facing him. One of the men pushes it towards him*]

THOMSON [*flatly*]: I only wanted to see you. And, you cowards, you won't even grant me that. You won't even face me. But I should have known.

SECOND GAS MASK: We don't want any speeches, we're not on parade now. Either sign that or see the ammunition dump go.

[THOMSON *takes a fountain pen out of his pocket and scrawls his signature across the demands. He will make his speech whatever happens*]

THOMSON: Look at you, look around you, look at yourselves, and I hope you remember your pathetic cowardice till your dying days –

GILZEAN: Away and blacken your bum.

[*Loud laughter*]

THOMSON: Oh yes, yes, but not one of you is capable of looking me in the eye, of staring me in the face, standing there man to man –

[TOPLIS *takes his handkerchief away*]

Huh, you again. I won't forget you. Who are you – tell me – who are you?

TOPLIS: . . . Whoever I want to be. And who are you . . . anymore?

[*Silence.* THOMSON *takes one last long look around at them.* GILZEAN, *with his hands over his face, parts them briefly to stick his tongue out at* THOMSON. THOMSON *turns and walks out, followed by some of the soldiers. The men remove their disguises*]

It's all over, boys.

[*All of the men, except the first and second* GAS MASKS *file out of the back door with* TOPLIS, STRANGE, GILZEAN, *the* GEORDIE, *the* HARD MAN, FRENCHIE *and the* RUSSIAN. GEORDIE *calls to the* GAS MASKS]

GEORDIE: See you again lads, eh?

[TOPLIS *hustles him out. The* SECOND GAS MASK *speaks with his usual sarcasm*]

SECOND GAS MASK: Aye sure . . .

FIRST GAS MASK: Back to nature . . .

103/3. EXT/INT. THOMSON'S OFFICE. DAY

[*We see* THOMSON *slumping towards the outer office, where* GUINNESS *is on the telephone and the* CORPORAL CLERK *sits*]

GUINNESS: Yes, well. That will no longer be necessary. Thank you.

[THOMSON *walks in, doesn't look at them, and is only interrupted in his flight for his own office by* GUINNESS]

Sir! *Sir*!

[THOMSON *finally stops by his door, but does not look back*]

A Brigadier-General Charlesworth, 19th Cavalry Hussars, telephoned sir – they are ready to move with a machine gun section at one hour's notice. Sir . . .

[THOMSON *leans his head against his door. Looks finally, but almost out of the corner of his eye*]

THOMSON: When . . . when did that message arrive, Guinness?

GUINNESS [*innocently*]: Oh, some time after you left, sir.

[THOMSON *looks away. The* CORPORAL CLERK *looks towards* GUINNESS, *who still looks the picture of innocence*]

THOMSON: . . . Ring back Brigadier-General Charlesworth and tell him . . . that it doesn't matter . . . that the hour has passed.

[THOMSON *opens the door to his room.* GUINNESS *continues, brightly*]

GUINNESS: And a further message from High Command, Sir, Brigadier-General Horwood. Three hundred and sixty men from the First Honourable Artillery Company will be arriving at eighteen hundred hours this evening –

[THOMSON *moves to get away, but . . .*]

– and the first Royal Welsh Fusiliers, plus the 22nd. Manchesters will be here no later than tomorrow morning.

[*Silence*]

. . . . Sir?

[THOMSON *doesn't look at him. He walks straight into his room. And closes the door*]

104/3. INT. ETAPLES HOTEL BEDROOM. NIGHT

[*We see* TOPLIS *in the hotel bedroom, dressing once more in the uniform of a brave Captain. The Private's uniform is tossed onto a chair.*

Behind him we see, on the bed, the perplexed FRENCH GIRL.

TOPLIS *turns away from the window having taken his monocle from out of his pocket, puts it into position and straightens up.*

At the bedside he reaches down and kisses her on the forehead, moves to the door, opens it and departs]

105/3. EXT. HOTEL/TOWN SQUARE. NIGHT

[*The celebrations are well in hand. Laughter. The French on their streets again.*

A couple of very young Privates watch the singing and dancing as TOPLIS *comes out.*

Both men salute and TOPLIS *returns their salute casually. As* TOPLIS *goes past the man nearest to him, he flicks out casually at the man's hair above his ears. It is a shade longer than allowed*]

TOPLIS: I see you've been letting your hair run riot too, Private.

[*He turns and smiles again. Both men laugh. And look admiringly after him as he goes. From the street we see the* FRENCH GIRL *at the bedroom window, watching* TOPLIS *as he walks through the crowded square. We see* TOPLIS *as he saunters along. Only the boarded-up windows and occasional broken-down door and signs of fire suggest the earlier wild violence. A group of French people watch the festivities. As* TOPLIS *does so, we see and hear many of the men, more than tipsy, around one large fire. They sing, as* TOPLIS *goes*]

SINGING MEN: Keep the home fires burning,
Though your hearts are yearning,
Though the boys are far away,
They dream of home.
There's a silver lining
Through the dark clouds shining.
Turn the dark clouds inside out,
Till the boys come home.

106/3. INT. STRACHAN'S QUARTERS. DAY

[*Without* STRACHAN, *but with a splendid meal completed.*

HORWOOD, ASSER, *the two commanding officers for the First Welch Fusiliers, and the Twenty-second Manchesters*]

FUSILIERS: They just melted away, sir. Met very little resistance, did we, Teddy?

MANCHESTERS: Hardly had to do anything – except be here. Mind you, trying to single out the ringleaders is proving rather tricky, sir.

HORWOOD [*grimly*]: Not to put too fine a point on it, it is in our best interests, and the interests of the war effort, to get these mutineers out of here as fast as possible. We can start shipping them out tomorrow.

MANCHESTER: Up the Line, sir?

HORWOOD: Good God, man, where else? These men are badly needed for the big show. Give them a few days up at Passchendaele and they'll either be dead, or damned glad to be alive. Eh, Alex?

ASSER: Yes, all this mutiny nonsense will soon be forgotten. One way or another.

FUSILIERS: Isn't it a bit dangerous though, sir, to do absolutely nothing? The attacks on the NCOs alone, the damage . . . the abuse . . . won't that encourage a repetition of these . . . events . . . Sir?

HORWOOD: Have you finished?

FUSILIERS: . . . Yes, sir.

HORWOOD: Good. Because my priority is the bloody deserters. Red flags were flown – *and we're not having that.* Bolsheviks and cowards – they're the ones I want, and that will be the first priority for the new Chief of Police, and that Secret Service chappie I've been hearing about . . . er . . .

[ASSER *picks up a paper off the table*]

ASSER: Woodhall. Edwin Woodhall. The best, from all accounts. The very best.

[*Smiles*]

But rather small.

107/3. EXT. SANCTUARY. WOODS. DAY

[*We see men hurtling through a wet and mist-marooned forest – a 'sanctuary' on the run. One or two are vaguely identifiable from previous scenes. We hear shouts and gunfire from behind them and then see a blur of policemen at either side.*

They are being driven into a trap, the GEORDIE *amongst the first.*

We see the clearing as the men emerge to face a group of Red Caps, guns raised, waiting for them. A truck is in the background.

The men are quickly surrounded and start to be led away, knackered. We see the figure later identified as WOODHALL *sitting in the driver's seat of a car, watching dispassionately. He doesn't seem, sitting down in the car, to be spectacularly small.*

All the deserters seem to have been captured. We see WOODHALL *finally climb out of his car. He has a piece of paper with him. And he is indeed small, but well formed.*

As WOODHALL *closes the car door we just catch sight of a cushion on his seat.*

He approaches the captured men, looking quickly but carefully at each one, and allows himself a small smile as he sees GILZEAN.]

109/3. INT. THOMSON'S OFFICE. DAY

[THOMSON *with* WOODHALL *in close up*]

WOODHALL: Gordon Highlander with an English accent.
[*Looks down at his notes*]
Average height. Brown hair – thick head of, high cheek bones, cruel face, except when he smiled . . . the smile, General.

THOMSON: He just seemed different, that's all. Like . . . suddenly someone else was in the car with me. I can't explain it any better than that. Oh well yes, I can – he looked like an officer when he smiled . . . Silly but . . .

WOODHALL: No, please do go on, sir.

THOMSON: Later, when I signed those demands – confidence, you know, something like that. Command. And my God, Woodhall, he was in charge of those men, young though he was, and the fools would have done anything for him.

WOODHALL: Thank you, General.
[*Stands*]
I will get an artist working on a representation of the man. I would be very grateful if you would look at it when it is finished.
[*For the first time, as* THOMSON *finishes, we move back from them and see the whole range of tea chests, sea chests and packing cases surrounding them*]

THOMSON: You'd better make it quick, hadn't you? I'm going to have an illness. So I've been told!

109A/3. INT. WHITEWASHED ROOM. DAY

[*We see a small whitewashed room, almost like an interrogation room.* WOODHALL *facing* THOMSON*'s driver from the scene where* TOPLIS *sits in the car. The man is polite but evasive*]

WOODHALL: Come on, you did see him. He got into the car.
THOMSON'S DRIVER: But he was just one of a crowd, and then he sat down in the back seat. So I don't know, Sergeant.
WOODHALL: But you must have some idea what he looked like.
[DRIVER *looks lost*]
Roughly.
THOMSON'S DRIVER [*helpfully*]: Well, he was taller than you, sergeant.

110/112/3. EXT. BEACH-SANCTUARY. DAY

[*We see* TOPLIS, *the* HARD MAN *and* STRANGE *on the edge of a beach, on the edge of some trees lining the coast. Sitting down, huddled up, perhaps half protected by some kind of part-camouflaged bivouac. Their haversacks are with them.*]

HARD MAN: . . . Christ, it's cold.
TOPLIS: I know.
HARD MAN: Worth risking a fire?
STRANGE: *No.*
HARD MAN [*looking around*]: We're going to get caught here. Either that or frozen.
[*Looks at* TOPLIS]
Didn't do us much good, did it, all that trouble?
TOPLIS: Oh I don't know, Franny.
HARD MAN: I do. And it didn't. If they'd chased the Germans like they've chased us since then, the bloody war would have been over long ago.
STRANGE: . . . I think we should go.
HARD MAN: But where?
STRANGE: Home.
HARD MAN: I'll send for a cab. The tram service around here is soddin' disgraceful.
STRANGE: Make our way to Boulogne, there's always a madness

there of the new and the wounded, thousands coming and going with every tide. Take our chances. What do you think, Percy?

TOPLIS: Can you get a boat from Boulogne to Russia?

STRANGE: I'm not a Bolshevik, and you know it. Are you coming or what?

TOPLIS: No – I will eventually, Charles, but not just yet. I think I'll stroll about for a while. See what's cooking.

HARD MAN: If anyone's cooking, Perce, it'll be you – you'll be the main course.

STRANGE: You're mad, you must be – if they're looking for anyone, it'll be you.

TOPLIS: Who me? Nah, I don't think so. What did I do? I just had a laugh, that's all . . . anyway, I like Army life.

[*The other two shake their heads and smile*]

And it'll be going dark soon, boys, better be making a move.

[*Silence.* TOPLIS *stares out, then they shake hands briefly. The* HARD MAN *takes his haversack and leaves the bivouac*]

STRANGE: I will remember what you did for me, you know – everything, Perce. I won't forget.

TOPLIS [*easily, flatly*]: Neither will I. 'Bye, Strange.

[*Winks*]

See you again sometime.

[STRANGE *ducks his head out of the bivouac.* HARD MAN *and* STRANGE *go off into the trees. We see* TOPLIS *alone, expressionless, as he undoes his haversack – and takes out another officer's tunic*]

113/3. INT. WHITEWASHED ROOM. DAY

[*We see the whitewashed room again. We hear* WOODHALL. *Persuasive. See the wizened small Corporal,* GILZEAN, *staring out, arm bandaged.*]

WOODHALL: . . . I bet you knew him really well, didn't you?

GILZEAN: Away to fuck.

WOODHALL: Next.

114/3. INT. SAME WHITEWASHED ROOM. LATER

GEORDIE: I shouldn't be here. I should be in hospital.
WOODHALL: Had a terrible war really, haven't you?
GEORDIE: Yes, yes, I bloody well have.
WOODHALL: All that can change.
GEORDIE [*sparking for a change*]: Oh aye I know, I can be shot for desertion. That'll make a change.

[WOODHALL *takes out a wanted poster with an artist's impression of* TOPLIS, *and puts it in front of the* GEORDIE. *He can see the financial reward, written in French and English money*]

WOODHALL: Long spell in hospital, that's what you need, I would think. In fact, I wouldn't be surprised if by the time you were fully recovered and ready to face charges, well, it could easily be after the end of the war. Peacetime. You don't get shot for desertion in peacetime.
GEORDIE [*head down*]: I don't want to die.
WOODHALL: I know you don't. It's not a pastime I would recommend. Especially not for someone like yourself, who has plainly suffered enough . . . Tell me about him.
GEORDIE: . . . He didn't start anything.
WOODHALL: We know that. We know who's really to blame.
GEORDIE [*in a rush*]: If you want to know, he was a hero. He didn't seem like one, or act like one, you never knew what he was thinking, or which way he would go, and you never even knew till it had happened. Like. And then you realized.
WOODHALL: I bet you knew him really well, didn't you?
GEORDIE: . . . Yes . . .

[WOODHALL *glances down at the* GEORDIE*'s records*]

WOODHALL: The autumn of '15, Loos Royal Army Medical Corp. Stretcher bearer? Wounded in action . . . Met him then, did you?

[*Finally the* GEORDIE *nods*]

Tell me his name. That's all . . . That's not a lot to ask, in return . . . *is it?*

115/3. EXT. ROAD NEAR BULLRING. DAY

[*The large notice board on the road facing the beach beside the deserted Bullring says 'Training Camp Number One'.*

We see the abandoned bayonet range; the empty gas hut.

Amongst the notices are a number of lists of deserters who are 'wanted'; and finally, an artist's impression on a poster offering two hundred pounds reward – for PERCY TOPLIS.

TOPLIS*'s hand removes the paper and crumples it. He walks off through the sand dunes*]

116/3. INT. LIBERTY HOTEL BAR. DAY
15 OCTOBER 1917

[TOPLIS *is in a hotel bar, monocled, officered, playing the piano. It is midday, there are few other customers.*

TOPLIS *plays 'Let the great big world keep turning'. Cigarette burning, drink on top of the piano*]

TOPLIS: If I knew that someone cared for me,
I'd let the world go by.
Someone who was true as true could be,
I'd never want to sigh.
What would I give today
Just to hear someone softly say,
Let the great big world keep turning,
Never mind if I've got you;
For I only know that I want you so,
And there's no one else will do.
You have simply set me yearning,
And for ever I'll be true.
Let the great big world keep on turning round,
Now I've found someone like you.

Love, they say, must come to one and all
Of high and low degree,
Come what may, I'm waiting for the call,
It holds no fears for me.
Maybe the day is near
When the thought of my heart I'll hear,
Let the great big world keep turning,
Never mind if I've got you;
For I only know that I want you so,
And there's no one else will do.

You have simply set me yearning,
And for ever I'll be true.
Let the great big world keep on turning round,
Now I've found someone like you.
[*Perhaps we hear him singing throughout the following sequences*]

117/3. EXT. VILLAGE CEMETERY. DAY

[*The cemetery at the western end of the village of Rang du Fliers, twelve kilometres south of Etaples.*

We see WOODHALL *by a large sepulchre.*

He takes from his bag a dog collar and begins to move behind the sepulchre, to exchange his clothing for those of an Army Chaplain. He loves every second of it.

In the background, waiting, bored, by their vehicle, are four of WOODHALL*'s 'new-style Military Police'*]

118/3. INT. LIBERTY HOTEL BAR. DAY

[*We see* TOPLIS *as he reaches the final verse of the song. Has been singing for himself and no others. The few French customers and occasional soldier barely notice.*

WOODHALL *enters, and walks towards the bar by the piano, listening to* TOPLIS *complete the song.*

TOPLIS *finishes singing, picks up his cigarette*]

WOODHALL [*Irish, of course*]: A fine sentiment, Captain. Beautifully played.
[TOPLIS *looks at him*]
I heard you from outside. Simply delightful. You don't know the Mountains of Mourne, do you?
TOPLIS: Not personally no.
WOODHALL [*laughs*]: Pity. A lovely song. Full of the mists of time. Can I buy you a drink?
[TOPLIS *for the first time weighs him up quickly*]
TOPLIS: I've just about finished, Padre.
WOODHALL: Oh, one more, surely, perhaps another song or two.
[WOODHALL *turns, goes towards* TOPLIS]
TOPLIS [*shakes his head*]: Got a train to catch.

WOODHALL: One for the road, what do you say – one for the train?
TOPLIS: No really.
WOODHALL: Oh don't be like that.
TOPLIS: I said 'no'.

[TOPLIS *begins to stand up. Glances for a back door*]

WOODHALL: I insist.

[*As he does so, he draws a gun, inches away from* TOPLIS*'s face. He produces a whistle and blows it hard. Four armed policemen burst in, and surround* TOPLIS]

TOPLIS [*flatly*]: All right, I'll have a drink.

119/3. INT. CAR APPROACHING DETENTION DAY

[*We see* TOPLIS *being driven through the Etaples Base Camp, approaching the prison compound with* WOODHALL, *two of the policemen and driver.*

WOODHALL *sits almost sideways so that he can see* TOPLIS *and enjoy the view.*

TOPLIS *appears to stare out stoically*]

WOODHALL [*grins*]: Yes, we executed our first mutineer yesterday. A good friend of yours, I'm sure . . . a chap called Gilzean . . . I expect they'll drop some of the other charges against you like 'impersonating an officer' – and such like.
TOPLIS: That's very decent of them . . .
WOODHALL: . . . All those stories about you . . .

[*Shakes his head*]

. . . looking at you now, you don't look much like a hero to me.
TOPLIS: That's the last thing I am . . . Cemeteries are full of heroes.
WOODHALL: Yes. Of course they're not so full of deserters, but they're there all the same. Hidden away in some corner, untended, uncared for, unloved.
TOPLIS: You'll say a prayer over me though, won't you, Padre?

[WOODHALL *enjoys the 'joke'. As we arrive at the prison compound*]

120/3. EXT. DETENTION COMPOUND. DAY

[TOPLIS *is led away. We see him quietly but anxiously looking around himself.*

'The prison was a stockade erected from huge wooden stakes about ten feet high, and inside this was a double row of barbed-wire entanglements surrounding several wooden guardhouses.'

TOPLIS *takes all of this in; the guards who escort him into the guardhouse are unarmed.*

WOODHALL *stands on the running board of his car*]

WOODHALL: See you tomorrow then, hey?
TOPLIS: Don't be late . . .

[TOPLIS *meets again the* WELSH NCO GUARD *he pistol whipped earlier in the episode*]

WELSH NCO GUARD: Hello son, remember me . . . ?

121/3. INT. DETENTION CELL AND CORRIDOR NIGHT

[*Late that evening.*

We see a badly beaten-up TOPLIS *in a small room occupied by one other prisoner – a man of somewhat ruffian appearance, the* HARD MAN*'s ugly brother.*

They are half lying, half sitting on their beds. Two chairs alongside. A wooden beam goes across the ceiling, about ten feet off the floor.

TOPLIS *finally focuses on the beam. For some time. As he does so, we hear a guard approaching. And a spy hole is opened. An eye looks in. The spy hole is closed. The guard marches on.*

TOPLIS *looks towards the sheets on his bed. Then back to the beam. He finally goes to sit beside his colleague*]

TOPLIS: How would you like to help me hang myself?
COLLEAGUE: I'm in enough trouble as it is.

[*We fade. We come back to the scene as we see* TOPLIS *sitting on his bed, quietly counting to himself. We hear the guard approaching. He stops at the door*]

TOPLIS: 64, 65, 66, 67, 68, 69, 70, 71, 72, 73, 74.

[*The spy hole is opened. An eye looks in. The spy hole is closed*]

74 again . . . they must wind this feller up . . .

[*We fade out. Fade back in. We see* TOPLIS *standing on the chair. Blanket strips torn into a rope, attached to his neck, going up towards, and tied to, the beam. His colleague moves in to hold the chair* TOPLIS *is standing on*]

[*Whispering*] – 64, 65, 66, 67, 68, 69 –

[*We hear faint footsteps*]

70, 71 –

[*They get louder*]

– 72, 73, 74 –

[*Not there yet.* TOPLIS *winces*]

seventy-five – come on – seventy-si – *now*!

[TOPLIS*'s colleague flicks the chair away as we hear the footsteps stop.* TOPLIS *hangs. The keyhole opens. An eye looks in. All within a second*]

WELSH NCO GUARD: Jesus Christ!

[*The keyhole closes. The colleague jumps up, grabs* TOPLIS*'s legs, grabs the chair.* TOPLIS *stands on it. The* GUARD, *who has been fumbling with his keys, opens the door. He dashes into the room and looks at* TOPLIS, *standing on the chair, arms folded*]

TOPLIS [*flatly*]: And for my next trick . . .

[TOPLIS *kicks the guard and his colleague hauls him silently and savagely to the floor*]

122/3. EXT. EDGE OF THE BARBED WIRE COMPOUND. THREE A.M.

[*We see* TOPLIS *and his colleague tunnelling furiously under the barbed wire.*

As they burrow themselves under, a searchlight finally hits them.

We hear shouts followed by rifle bullets. But they are gone]

123/3. INT. WOODHALL'S QUARTERS. NIGHT

[WOODHALL *at his bureau.*

We see his diary. He is completing a beautifully handwritten description of his brave capture of PERCY TOPLIS.

He leans back in his chair, content]

124/3. EXT. COUNTRY LANE. DERBYSHIRE. DAY LATE SUMMER, 1918. A YEAR LATER

[*We see a country lane. Signposts for Nottingham and Derby. Stone walls either side.*

It is deserted except for a motor car and an attractive lady, DOROTHY.

The bonnet of the car is up. Steam rising – from the car and DOROTHY.

She has her back turned as TOPLIS *approaches, walking, suitcase in hand. Perhaps a moustache in place above his lip, civilian clothes.*

We see him looking at the lady and the car. She kicks the car. We see him approaching a gate, disappearing into the field.

We see TOPLIS *emerge from the field in military best. Suitcase in hand, monocle in place.*

He saunters towards the car. And DOROTHY]

125/3. INT. RESTAURANT. NIGHT

[*We see* TOPLIS *and* DOROTHY *in a fashionable corner of a fashionable restaurant.*

Expensive food and wine, with a waiter to match. Music and laughter and TOPLIS *in full mimicry and mannerisms. We can see that* DOROTHY *is caught between fascination and giggles.*

We also see that DOROTHY *is in her early thirties, a stunningly beautiful woman.*

Fine clothes, fine manners but perhaps a hint of something wild as in 'wilderness'.

The waiter approaches with the wine. He pours it and TOPLIS *tastes. Being important, he doesn't like it, shakes his head*]

WAITER: Very sorry, sir.

[*He moves away*]

TOPLIS: . . . And you must remember this, Dorothy, we were on the point of a major offensive. And there *he* was – Galloping through No Man's Land – with his hounds 'Tally-Ho'. Of course we asked him what the hell he was doing there. He said 'I'm looking for fox holes, dear boy. What else does a gentleman do at the weekend?'

[DOROTHY *laughs*]

126/3. EXT. RIVERSIDE. NIGHT

[*Dreamlike. And close up.*

We see TOPLIS *and* DOROTHY *dancing. The music has continued. They flaunt at each other. Closely.*

But completely alone. They are on the bridge over a river.

Gaslight and moonlight]

127/128/129/3. EXT. DOROTHY'S HOUSE AND ROAD NEARBY. NIGHT

[*A taxi waiting at the bottom of a driveway.*

At the top of the driveway is a cottage-style house of some expense and small grandeur.

All the curtains are drawn.

TOPLIS *and* DOROTHY *are standing in the middle of the driveway*]

TOPLIS: Yes, in tea, you see – for some time I thought they lived in a teapot.

[*They both laugh*]

Shall I send him away?

DOROTHY: No . . . The butler would never understand.

TOPLIS: You mean he doesn't know you've got a long-lost brother?

DOROTHY: No . . . And neither do I.

TOPLIS: An aged aunt perhaps.

DOROTHY: No. No, Johnny. It's not that. I've told you. My husband was . . .

TOPLIS: The dead don't know. I've seen enough to tell you that.

DOROTHY: It's just . . . I promised myself. That I wouldn't . . . 'entertain' anyone else in this house. His house.

TOPLIS: It's your house now.

[DOROTHY *shakes her head,* TOPLIS *nods and walks away*]

DOROTHY: . . . Johnny . . .

[*He turns around*]

Double three double four. Telephone me . . . Telephone me first . . . that is, if you want to.

TOPLIS: I'll do more than that. At midday tomorrow, young lady, I shall, with almost military precision, be outside whoever's house this is –

[*She looks at him quickly*]

– and I shall drive you either east or west –

DOROTHY: Or totally insane.

TOPLIS: I thought I'd done that already, must be slipping – but whichever way I drive you – east or west – mad or weak at the knees – I shall have you at the coast by teatime.

DOROTHY [*mock innocently*]: And what will happen then, Johnny . . . ?

TOPLIS: *I* shall entertain you.

[*Leans towards her and kisses her on the cheek*]

Goodnight.

[*He walks towards the taxi. We see* TOPLIS *at the rear door to the taxi. At first the smiles of pleasure and achievement, but the smile goes. And we see for the first time that he appears to be wistful and hesitant. Finally he climbs into the taxi.*

We hear a voice call out 'Mrs Taylor'. We see DOROTHY *glance first towards the driveway. The taxi has gone. We see two men appear from the shadows at the side of the house. They approach with an official envelope.* DOROTHY *takes the envelope and walks to the front door*]

129A/3. INT. TAXI. NIGHT

[*We see* TOPLIS *in the taxi.*

The driver is watching him in the mirror]

DRIVER'S VOICE: Had a good night, sir?

TOPLIS: . . . I had a . . . I don't know.

[*Laughs. Looks at the driver. He hands him his fobwatch*]

Out of curiosity, driver, how much would you give me for this . . . ?

130/3. INT. HOTEL BEDROOM. NIGHT

[DOROTHY *and* TOPLIS *completing some good wholesome fun and games.* TOPLIS *picks up a glass of wine, offers it to* DOROTHY *and drinks himself*]

DOROTHY: . . . You can entertain me for as long as you like, Johnny.

[*He grins*]

And when do you go away?

131/3. INT. THE FLYING HORSE HOTEL NOTTINGHAM. ARMISTICE DAY, 1918. DAY

[Noise of massive mid-afternoon celebrations outside. Church bells, people waving Union Jacks and cheering.

The hotel is crowded with men celebrating; a newspaper boy doing the rounds; a group round a piano singing 'Pack up your troubles'.

We see a man hidden by the paper he is reading. He reads the back page. The front page proclaims victory, etc. He lowers the newspaper. We see it is, predictably, TOPLIS, *dressed in the civilian clothes he wore when he first saw* DOROTHY. *A suitcase is at his side, a half pint, drained, on the table.*

He looks around at the scene. Notes, amid the excitement, some former soldiers, with one or two medals.

And at a nearby table, he sees a young man dressed and bedecked in an officer's uniform, a Mons Star, a number of Chevrons, another medal and an air of quiet conceit as he collects drinks from several sources]

GROUP [*sing*]: Pack up your troubles in your old kit bag
And smile, smile, smile,
While you've got a lucifer to light your fags,
Smile, boys, that's the style,
What's the use of worrying?
It never was worthwhile,
So pack up your troubles in your old kit bag
And smile, smile, smile.

Private Perks is a funny little codger
With a smile – a funny smile.
Five feet nine, he's an artful little dodger
With a smile – a sunny smile,
Flush or broke, he'll have his little joke,
He can't be suppressed.
All the other fellows have to grin,
When he gets this off his chest.

So pack up your troubles in your old kit bag
And smile, smile, smile,
While you've got a lucifer to light your fags,
Smile, boys, that's the style,
What's the use of worrying?
It never was worthwhile,

So pack up your troubles in your old kit bag
And smile, smile, smile.

[TOPLIS *folds his paper up, picks up his suitcase and approaches the table where the officer is. He sits down at his side, sideways on, and whispers in his ear*]

TOPLIS: Give me a sovereign.

THE MONS STAR: I beg your pardon.

TOPLIS: You heard. Give me a sovereign. *Now.*

[THE MONS STAR *looks around, hesitating about raising his voice*]

THE MONS STAR: Damned cheek.

TOPLIS: I know you have – but listen, if you're going to do something, pal, do it well.

[*Points*]

You've got a red chevron missing and your medal ribbon's back to front. Some soldier you must be. Now give me that sovereign before I scream the place down. And give me the Mons Star as well, I haven't got that one.

[MONS STAR *takes out a sovereign and gives it to* TOPLIS. TOPLIS *waits. The* MONS STAR *gives him the Mons Star*]

And polish y' boots and all, while y' at it.

[TOPLIS *picks up his suitcase and slides away towards the hotel exit – as a whisky arrives at the* MONS STAR*'s table*]

132/3. EXT. ROAD AND THE DRIVEWAY TO DOROTHY'S HOUSE. DAY

[TOPLIS *is dressed as an officer again. He draws up in a taxi outside the entrance to* DOROTHY*'s house.*

She comes out with a suitcase]

DOROTHY: Where have you been this time?

TOPLIS: Sorry I'm late.

DOROTHY: I don't mind the minutes, Johnny – it's the weeks.

TOPLIS: Ask no questions, and you'll be told no lies . . .

[*They look shyly at each other.* DOROTHY *picks up her suitcase, hands it to* TOPLIS. *He looks towards the house*]

If you're going to see ghosts, Dorothy, you'll see them wherever we go.

DOROTHY: No, no, no, it's not that, it's not him, believe me.

TOPLIS: Well, what is it then?

DOROTHY [*lightly*]: Ask no questions and . . .

[*We see* TOPLIS *and* DOROTHY *as they walk towards the taxi waiting at the bottom of the driveway, arm in arm*]

TOPLIS: All right, but I'm telling you, get rid of that ghost now, or he'll never let you go . . .

133/3. INT. THE FLYING HORSE HOTEL NOTTINGHAM. THE SAME DAY

[*A similar scene – except that the table where the* MONS STAR *has been sitting has been kicked over.*

People are standing up, shocked.

The MONS STAR, *lying face down, looks up and stares at a very small chauffeur, complete with cap and gloves, boots and jacket, holding a gun in his hand.*

It is WOODHALL, *of course.*]

FADE OUT

EPISODE 4
DEAD MAN ON LEAVE

134/4. EXT. LAKE. DAY

[TOPLIS *is relaxing in the stern of a rowing boat. He is reading a newspaper.* DOROTHY *is rowing.*

TOPLIS*'s attention is drawn to an article in the newspaper. He barely concentrates on what she is saying. At first.*]

DOROTHY: I've got a name for you, you know.
TOPLIS: You're not the only one.
DOROTHY: A special name. Late at night when I'm thinking of you, when inevitably you're not there, you're not Johnny Walker to me.
TOPLIS: I'm Gordon's Gin.
[DOROTHY *laughs. Comes closer to him*]
DOROTHY: No, you're 'sometimes'. My 'Mr Sometimes'. I was going to call you 'Mr One Weekend in Five, plus the Odd Unexpected Tuesday Night If I'm Really Lucky' – but –
TOPLIS: Go down well in High Society.
[*Butler's voice*]
'Who shall I say is calling, sir?'
[*Pause*]
I've never been invited inside your house, Dorothy – all this time and every daft excuse under the sun . . . I'm not complaining, but I haven't . . .
[TOPLIS *looks at the article in the newspaper*]
. . . so don't start on me.
DOROTHY: All right but . . . Don't go, please don't go this time . . . whatever the reasons . . . do you hear me?
TOPLIS: Funny you should say that. I've just found out I have to go to London.

DOROTHY: Why?

TOPLIS: There's a by-election in Southwark. And Labour are expected to win.

[*He grins at her*]

136/4. INT. HOTEL BEDROOM. DAWN

[TOPLIS *and* DOROTHY, *alone in a hotel bedroom.*

DOROTHY *is in bed.*

TOPLIS *is dressed. He picks up his suitcase and goes to the door*]

DOROTHY: And what will you do after you've been to London?

TOPLIS: Come back and see you. I won't be long.

[*She looks at him sceptically*]

Not this time.

[DOROTHY *shrugs. They both smile*]

DOROTHY: . . . There may not be anyone there to pay the bill . . . at six in the morning.

TOPLIS: That's not a problem.

DOROTHY: But I – I haven't . . .

TOPLIS: I paid it last night.

[*Another smile – from* TOPLIS. *He touches his lips. A small move. As if to blow the smallest of kisses*]

DOROTHY [*flatly, yet again*]: You're married, aren't you?

TOPLIS: No. No, I'm not married. I just wish it was as difficult as that. Don't forget – *I* will see you. Soon.

[*He goes out. Leaving her puzzled and then angry*]

DOROTHY: Dog! . . . Woof . . . Woof . . .

[*Pulls the bedclothes up and growls quietly*]

137/4. EXT/INT. DOROTHY'S HOUSE. NIGHT

[TOPLIS *climbs into front room of the house. Through the window.*

We see the interior of a house. A house of some size, but completely stripped of any furniture or suggestion of life.

And we see TOPLIS, *dressed as he was in the previous scene, suitcase by the window, as he walks from the front room through to the hall till finally he comes to a lounge.*

We see an easy chair, with a telephone and an ash tray on the floor.

TOPLIS *looks around, finally nods to himself and smiles, as if at last, the pieces of the puzzle have fallen into place.*

He takes out his monocle and puts it on the arm of the chair.

He starts to leave the room]

138/4. EXT. BLACKWELL COLLIERY AND VILLAGE. STILL NOVEMBER, 1919. DAY

[*A lorry approaches the colliery.* TOPLIS *is in the back. He stops the lorry, gets out, and walks up the hill by the colliery.*

We see him walking through the village of Blackwell, toward ANNIE *and* FRANK WEBSTER*'s house.*

TOPLIS, *small suitcase in hand, is approaching a fierce and loud argument between two women, aged about thirty.*

There is a small crowd around them some of the time – until the argument becomes a fight. We may hear snatches of 'conversation' as TOPLIS *approaches, passes and continues towards the* WEBSTERS' *house*]

FIRST FEMALE: Kitty Harrison, come here.

SECOND FEMALE: Out me way.

FIRST FEMALE: I said I want a word with you.

SECOND FEMALE: What for?

[*We may hear snatches of 'conversation' as* TOPLIS *approaches, passes and continues towards the* WEBSTERS' *house*]

FIRST FEMALE: You know what I'm talking about. It's his!

SECOND FEMALE: It's not!

FIRST FEMALE: Well it were his!

SECOND FEMALE: But it's not now – it's mine!

FIRST FEMALE: Not when I've finished with you, it won't be.

[*The two women throw themselves at each other, like fighting hens. They scratch and crash and bite and pull and butt and punch each other to the floor. They roll out of the small crowd and towards* TOPLIS. *Finally, the* FIRST FEMALE *gets the* SECOND FEMALE *pinned to the floor, her knees holding the other one's shoulders to the floor.*

TOPLIS *walks round them*]

Listen girl, so far I've been sodding polite to you.

[*As he does so, his* AUNTIE ANNIE, *at her door, sees* TOPLIS]

ANNIE: Percy.

[ANNIE *hurries towards* TOPLIS, *takes hold of him and embraces him. Behind them, people are finally pulling the two women apart. Limb from limb*]

TOPLIS: What's all that about?

ANNIE: Oh, the usual. Mary Turner's husband went to war. And when he came back, Kitty Harrison had his job.

TOPLIS [*as he goes in*] There's a lot of it about. In fact, I'd go as far as to say it's an epidemic.

139/4. INT. WEBSTERS' LIVING ROOM AND KITCHEN. DAY

[ANNIE, *now in her mid-forties, looks in her mid-fifties.*

FRANK, *of a similar age, looks nearly dead, huddled in a chair by the fire, smoking and coughing*]

FRANK: Aye, well, it's the lungs. Isn't it? The bloody coal . . . Some fancy name they've come up with. Means yer lungs're buggered.

[*We see* TOPLIS, *also sat by the fire. Cake on a plate, tea on his lap.* ANNIE *sits on a hard-backed chair by the small dining table*]

TOPLIS: So what will you do?

FRANK: I don't know. I were thinking of sailing around the world. Me and the Aga Khan.

TOPLIS [*grinning*]: But Douglas Fairbanks stepped in.

FRANK [*flatly*]: I know. Still, 's' all right though – while he's away, he's leavin' me Mary Pickford.

ANNIE: She's upstairs now.

[*They all smile.* FRANK *coughs*]

FRANK: So, anyroads up, what is tha' doing here, 'Captain'? Long time no see.

TOPLIS [*as an officer*]: I had a war to win, Uncle Frank.

FRANK: Bloody war's been over nigh on a year.

TOPLIS: I know – the country just couldn't do without me. I kept saying, I said to old Haig and Lloyd George many a time, I said, 'Listen gentlemen, my Auntie Annie and my Uncle Frank, they'll be missing me,' but . . .

ANNIE [*lightly*]: Thy mother's been missing thee.

TOPLIS: How could she – she never noticed me when I were there.

You'd have had to call me Johnny Walker and distil me first.

ANNIE: She's been poorly.

TOPLIS: Another bad fall, was it – late at night, down the steps of the Old Dog and Garter?

ANNIE: She's nearly blind and all on her own.

[TOPLIS *stands up, is politely gentle*]

TOPLIS: You took me in, Auntie Annie, you know why . . . Listen. I may not have been much of a son to you –

[*He grins*]

– one way or another, but you're the only parents I ever had.

[*He approaches* FRANK *as he talks. Pats him on the shoulder*]

Look after yourself.

[*Then shouts up the stairs*]

He'll be up in a minute, Mary!

[TOPLIS *turns to the front door.* ANNIE *goes with him.* FRANK*'s mild laughter has turned to terminal coughing.* ANNIE *closes the door behind herself. They stand outside*]

How is he really?

ANNIE: As bad as can be expected. He'll not work again. I suppose there's lots of younger men could say the same, with unemployment as it is . . . but at least they can get about – they can breathe.

TOPLIS: So he doesn't get out much?

ANNIE: Not at all.

TOPLIS: Then he won't be needin' his bike then, Auntie Annie?

ANNIE: Do you mean the bike he bought to replace the one you stole?

[TOPLIS *acknowledges this with his raised forefinger*]

TOPLIS: The very one.

ANNIE: Well, it's an improvement, I suppose – at least you asked this time. I was going to sell it.

TOPLIS: I was going to buy it. Just as soon as . . . times are hard, Annie . . . But I've recently found out that this wartime companion of mine just made good. I predicted as much myself so I thought I'd cycle down to London and share his good fortune for a while. And I'm in love now as well.

ANNIE: Aye – and what've tha' stolen off her? Go on, get off with th' – I'll see thee the next time tha' wants something.

[*A small pause*]

Go on, take the bike. Send us the money when tha' can. But on one condition.

[*She looks at him*]

TOPLIS: Look, I ain't seen my mam proper in thirteen years. Why now?

ANNIE: Because she's tha' mam. Tha' proper mam.

TOPLIS: I'll go and get the bike.

[*He leaves her.* ANNIE *stands in the doorway*]

140/4. EXT. MAM'S STREET. DAY

[*We see* TOPLIS *cycling along, suitcase on the back of the bike, at the edge of the village, approaching a final row of small houses, run down and bleak.*

He glances across at one house in particular. Near the end of the row. Then rides straight past it for a few yards, before finally getting off the bike]

141/4. EXT. DOORWAY AND INT TOPLIS'S MOTHER'S HOUSE. DAY

[*We see true poverty, whatever the circumstances or causes. Below-the-breadline furniture and facilities. A home of some despair and disrepair.*

Yet we hear a surprisingly beautiful, if gin-stained woman's voice, singing a version of 'If you were the only girl in the world' to and for herself alone]

MAM: . . . If you were the only boy in the world,
And I was the only girl,
Nothing else would matter in the world today,
We would go on loving in the same old way . . .

[*As we hear her, we take in the scene.* TOPLIS *at the door, his suitcase still in his hand. And his* MOTHER, *who could pass for sixty. Her clothes are virtual rags, but lots of them, as she sits by a near dead fire. On the hearth above the fireplace, we see the picture taken of* TOPLIS *during his return to Blackwell as a war hero*]

. . . A garden of Eden just made for two,
With nothing to mar our joy,
There would be such wonderful things to do,
I would –

[TOPLIS*'s* MAM *stops singing. Half turns awkwardly from the fire, towards the door*]

There's someone there, who's there? Come on, I can feel the cold, the door's open . . . is it thee, Annie? . . . Annie?

[TOPLIS *hesitates at the door, almost goes away. His* MAM *approaches near blindly*]

Who are thee, are th' a man?

TOPLIS [*coughs*]: Ah, Mrs Toplis, isn't it?

MAM: Who are thee – there's nothing here.

TOPLIS: I'm . . . a doctor, Doctor . . . Walker.

MAM: I didn't send for the doctor. I can't afford a doctor.

TOPLIS: No, no, it's free – this one is free. A free visit. I'm new around here, you see. Trying to drum up some business.

MAM: Is the medicine free?

TOPLIS: Well, no, but –

MAM: Just as well, otherwise tha'd be bankrupt with me alone!

[*A coarse laugh*]

Well, come in then, lad, and shut the door.

[*Again,* TOPLIS *briefly hesitates, then enters, closing the door. He puts his suitcase and hat on the table, puts in his monocle and approaches his* MAM *as she goes to sit in the chair*]

TOPLIS: Well, any complaints?

MAM: I don't like the man next door.

[*She laughs.* TOPLIS *grins finally*]

TOPLIS: Health complaints, Mrs Toplis.

MAM: It is a health complaint – he makes me sick.

[*More laughter*]

TOPLIS: Your sister-in-law, Mrs . . .

[*Flicks his fingers*]

MAM: Webster. Annie Webster.

TOPLIS: Annie Webster – she says you hadn't been at all well. Would –

MAM: Where's tha' stethoscope?

TOPLIS: Oh I think we'll save that for now.

MAM: Till I have to pay for its use.

TOPLIS [*laughs*]: Just tell me, how have you been?

MAM [*soberly*]: Aye well, my eyes have gone, and my bowels are well buggered up. But I can't afford the medicine, so don't bother.

[*Tries to focus on* TOPLIS]

Is that a whatsitsname there?

TOPLIS: A monocle?

MAM: Mm.

TOPLIS: Yes, it is. Took one in the eye, you know, shrapnel, during the war. Bit dicky since.

MAM: My son was in the war. He was a hero. That's him up there on the mantelpiece.

TOPLIS: What a strange place to sit.

[*She laughs.* TOPLIS *moves to the mantelpiece to look at the photograph*]

. . . A captain, by the look of him.

MAM: Yes, he's dead now.

[TOPLIS *looks totally shocked for a second*]

Well, come on then, at least tha' can feel my pulse.

[MAM *holds her hand out to* TOPLIS, *frail and not completely clean.* TOPLIS *finally takes hold of* MAM *by the wrist. Holds her, stares at her for some seconds, holding his mother's hand, and yet not*]

TOPLIS: This boy of yours, how did he die, Mrs Toplis?

MAM: Very bravely . . .

[TOPLIS *stays holding his* MOTHER*'s wrist. Waiting. Finally she nods*]

Very bravely indeed . . . if tha' stays down on your knees holding my hand much longer, young man, I'll take it as a proposal of marriage.

[*And the same coarse laughter, as* TOPLIS *releases her hand*]

TOPLIS: A fine pulse, Mrs . . .

MAM: Toplis.

TOPLIS: Yes, see you well through the winter, that pulse will.

MAM: I hope so . . . I'm forty-three, tha' knows. Don't tha' want to know that, for tha' records?

TOPLIS: The next time, Mrs Toplis. The next time.

[*He stands up.* MAM *'looks' up at* TOPLIS]

MAM: Is that it?

TOPLIS: Certainly is.

MAM [*sniffs up*]: Good job it was free then . . . Are tha' sure I don't know thee, lad?

TOPLIS: Absolutely . . . I've just arrived here. And I'll just be going . . .

MAM: How much do th' charge then?

TOPLIS: Oh, the . . . standard rate.

MAM: Gin's cheaper.

TOPLIS: But is it wiser?

MAM: Nothing to live for – so, does it matter? God knows, I've had nothing to live for since my only boy died.

[*For a second we see pure hatred snarling through* TOPLIS*'s face – to be changed just as suddenly to near tears*]

TOPLIS: Goodbye. Mrs Toplis.

[MAM *doesn't answer him. He turns and reaches the door. She starts humming. He opens the door, looks back, then closes it and stays in the room as his mother starts singing again, just for herself*]

MAM: Nothing else would matter in the world today,
We would go on loving in the same old way,
A garden of Eden –

[TOPLIS *turns and opens the door again. He slams it behind him*]

Doctor Walker?

142/4. EXT. COUNTRY LANE. DAY

[*We see* TOPLIS *cycling along a long and winding country lane. Woods and thick brush are on one side of the road.*
Another man with him, another suitcase]

CYCLIST: . . . It's a long way away.
TOPLIS: Aye.
CYCLIST: Luton'll do me. I heard there's work in Luton.
TOPLIS: That's all there'll be.

[*The cyclist smiles. They look up. There is a flurry of movement, of beating and shouting from the trees and brush, some distance to their side. A flock of pheasants fly into the air. A crash of gunfire follows them. Both men throw themselves off their bikes. A pheasant comes hurtling down, almost hitting one of them. Both the cyclist and* TOPLIS *look at each other, then at the bird. Then they try to take the pheasant with them, and two suitcases. Like a silent movie, till* TOPLIS *sits on the pheasant on the saddle of his bike and they ride off*]

I hope it's dead, its beak's up my arse . . .

143/4. EXT. WOODS. NIGHT

[*We see them at nightfall in the woods. A cold and frosty night.*
The pheasant is on a makeshift spit above a fire, plucked and looking well done]

CYCLIST: Aye, two leg wounds, one medal and no job when I come home. That's why I'm here – wife's goin' loopy, and it's understandable – this is the least I could do. For her . . . and the kids . . . You got anyone, Lawrence? Family an' that?

TOPLIS: I'm . . . I've found someone I really . . . you know.
[*Smiles warmly and then looks away*]
CYCLIST: Oh. What's her name?
TOPLIS: Dorothy. She's had money in her time. And I've got to get some . . .
CYCLIST: What do you reckon?
TOPLIS: If it gets any smaller, we'll be eatin' wood pigeon.
CYCLIST: If there's nothin' for me in Luton, I'm re-enlisting, bad as it is.
[*The* CYCLIST *takes the pheasant off the spit and pulls it apart*]
TOPLIS: Till there's another war.
CYCLIST: Oh there won't be another war. *That* was the great war. There won't be any more. Not like that.
TOPLIS: Of course there won't, not till the next madman or king or capitalist says so. Not till the next national or financial crisis. Not till –
[*Stops himself, laughs*]
– it's all right though, I was thinking of re-enlisting myself – after all, it could be ages yet before we're cannon fodder again.
CYCLIST: You're not one of them socialists, are you?
TOPLIS: No, but I used to know one. Once.
[*They bite into the pheasant*]
CYCLIST: Hey, this is all right!
TOPLIS: I know, but have you any idea what it tastes like when those rich bastards in their manor houses have it, when it's been left to hang in a cellar for days on end, roasted and spiced, sauce and sauté potatoes, wine and silver and chandeliers . . . totally different.
CYCLIST: Oh . . . what does it taste like?
TOPLIS: Shite.

144/4. INT. MRS TOPLIS' HOUSE. NIGHT

[MRS TOPLIS*'s hovel.*
We see ANNIE WEBSTER *and* MRS TOPLIS.
MRS TOPLIS *is crying, near to hysterics.*
As ANNIE WEBSTER *bitterly tries to comfort her*]

145/146/4. EXT/INT. DOROTHY'S HOUSE NIGHT

[DOROTHY, *alone, sitting looking out, smoking a cigarette.*
A telephone is on the floor.
The chair is the only piece of furniture in the room.
TOPLIS*'s monocle is on her lap. She brings down her hand and holds it*]

147/4. INT. ASSEMBLY HALL. NIGHT

[*As large and as crowded as possible.*
Banners, a head table, a small stage.
A committee, and CHARLES STRANGE, *prospective MP for the constituency.*
He is approaching the end of the kind of passionate, bracing, embracing, moving speech he was incapable of in 1917.
Without a trace of a stammer. And then we also see EDWIN WOODHALL, *near the front of the hall, amongst a row of journalists.*
He too makes notes as STRANGE *speaks*]

STRANGE: – and they marched, brothers, they marched not for money nor jobs, nor against the wealthy or for fear of the workhouse, but they marched in bitter remembrance of Armistice Day, just a year gone by and so already have the hopes and dreams of those returning heroes!
[*We see* TOPLIS, *standing in the shadows at the back of the hall. He allows himself a small grin on 'returning heroes'*]
And if you were there, as I was there, you will know the numbers, and you will know that ten thousand marched, and you will also know that the capitalist newspapers never saw fit to print that news. News of ten thousand men and more, coming out of that grey mist of a November morning, approaching the Cenotaph, the wail of the fifes from the marching bands, the measured tread of tramping men, their war medals hanging from red banners and their pawn tickets pinned to their coats.
[*As he talks, we see that men in the hall have performed a similar act, red flags waving, many men with pawn tickets pinned to their coats*]
– A silent indictment against a system which praises the dead and condemns the living to starvation. And at the head of that

procession, they carried a large wreath with an inscription, that read: 'From the living victims – the unemployed – to our dead comrades who died in vain.'

[*He is near to whispering, the crowd is in his hands.* WOODHALL *exchanges glances with the fellow snoop at the side of him*]

And they lay that wreath where all the other wreaths lay, and yes they played 'The Dead March' and then 'Auld Lang Syne', but my God, I'll tell you this, we finished off with 'The Red Flag' and 'The Internationale'

[*Applause*]

and then, with quickened step, the living heroes passed out of Whitehall on their way back . . . to their cold and hungry homes . . .

[*He brings his voice up again, slowly, to reach a vivid climax*]

And brothers and sisters, my Conservative opponents – and every Conservative newspaper in the land – asks 'Why all this unrest, why these protests? What ails the common workers?'

[*Smiles*]

And I will tell you what I will tell them when I am voted into Parliament on your behalf – I will tell of those who laid down their lives for a land fit for heroes,

['*Hear Hear's*]

I will tell of the two million unemployed in this land fit for heroes – I will tell of the poverty and slums where there should not be one hungry mouth to feed in this land fit for heroes

[*Applause*]

and I will demand changes, I will demand them in the name of working-class solidarity against the capitalist war mongers and profiteers!

[*Applause*]

And only then, *only then* will we have a land fit for heroes!

[*Applause, thunderous and deserved. He holds his hands high, to a standing ovation, as the 'Red Flag' is played by a small band. He begins to move through the hall, being mobbed and greeted as he goes, and given protection by a small group of 'minders'. We see* WOODHALL *finishing his notes. Sitting down. Glancing at* STRANGE *as he goes past, then losing sight of him in the standing crowd surrounding him. And we see* STRANGE *as he approaches the back of the hall, going completely out of* WOODHALL*'s vision. And* TOPLIS *moves forward, moves to* STRANGE*'s side*]

TOPLIS: Hello, Strange . . .

[*And* STRANGE *immediately reveals the slightest of stammers*]

STRANGE: P . . . Percy! By Christ, man!

[STRANGE *reaches past his minders, and hugs him immediately and warmly*]

TOPLIS [*as he is hugged*]: 'Brother', surely.

STRANGE: What are you doing here – *how are you?*

[*Turns to one of the minders*]

John, this man – this man . . .

[TOPLIS *shakes his head, holds his hands out in protest*]

TOPLIS: Charles, no, no, not tonight, don't talk about me in a land fit for heroes.

[*They both grin. People begin to mass around them*]

Just give me ten minutes, somewhere – alone.

STRANGE: Of course.

[STRANGE *nods to his 'minders'. They all begin to move away, crowded in, towards a door leading off the main body of the hall. As the minders begin to move away, we see* WOODHALL *now almost alone in his seat.* WOODHALL, *twisted around in his chair, cannot, because of the crowds, see* TOPLIS *and* STRANGE. WOODHALL*'s fellow snoop leans across to him*]

FELLOW SNOOP: We've got every exit covered, sir, but what about his men around him?

WOODHALL: Two of them are mine.

[WOODHALL, *as is his wont, smiles happily*]

148/4. INT. SMALL ROOM. CORRIDOR NIGHT

[*A room with the usual two doors on opposite walls*]

TOPLIS: Yes. This will do.

[TOPLIS *and* STRANGE *are alone, as one door closes and we briefly see a couple of 'minders' protecting their privacy. They sit down*]

STRANGE: So what was wrong with the other rooms?

TOPLIS: Oh you know me, Charles – I always like to have options. A way in and a way out. It's a habit of mine.

STRANGE: Are you er . . . running?

TOPLIS [*shakes his head*]: No, I play the odd game of football, but . . . What happened to the stammer?

STRANGE: I made it go away. And I paid someone to make it go away.

TOPLIS: That's a very sound policy.

STRANGE: So what have you been doing?

TOPLIS [*easily*]: Sweet FA, struggling. What else is there to do – apart from save mankind. And you're already doing that.

STRANGE: You could join me.

TOPLIS: No, no thanks – the decency of it'd kill me.

[TOPLIS *and* STRANGE *laugh.* STRANGE, *despite himself*]

STRANGE: All right. But . . . what do you want?

TOPLIS [*evenly*]: A hundred pounds, Charles.

STRANGE: *Pardon?*

TOPLIS [*shrugs*]: Granted.

STRANGE: *Off me?*

[TOPLIS *nods*]

Why?

TOPLIS: Because you're somebody now. And you can stand it. And because I'm in debt, and I'm in love.

[*Raises his eyebrows, and grins*]

STRANGE: I wouldn't have thought the latter was possible.

TOPLIS: I don't want your philosophy – I just want your money.

STRANGE: And what happens if I don't?

TOPLIS: I'll do something really really . . . despicable.

STRANGE: You would as well, wouldn't you?

TOPLIS [*flatly*]: 'Course I would. If you say so.

[STRANGE *rises*]

STRANGE: But Percy, don't you realize, can't you see – I would have *given* it to you, all you had to do was ask. And I would have given it to you. Why didn't you?

TOPLIS: *Because life's not like that, Strange.*

[*Pause.* STRANGE *gropes for his cheque book and pen, and finally throws it down on the table*]

STRANGE: You will accept a cheque, won't you?

TOPLIS: Oh come on, Charles, you know I trust you.

[STRANGE *flurries through writing a cheque. Flicks it away*]

STRANGE: This is goodbye, isn't it?

TOPLIS: Believe me, I shall never darken your destiny ever again.

[*He walks towards the door*]

You were very good in there, you know. In fact, you were . . . great. A great man. You even had me convinced . . . almost.

[STRANGE *approaches* TOPLIS *as* TOPLIS *opens the back door*]

STRANGE: Perce . . .

[TOPLIS *turns around and gets hit straight in the mouth by the kind of wild but clumsy haymaker thrown by the kind of man who has never hit anyone in his adult life.* TOPLIS *reels backwards out of the room into the corridor. The two 'minders' look stunned.* TOPLIS *holds his mouth, mumbles*]

TOPLIS: You pacifists are all the same.

[STRANGE *looks after him. Nobody is amused*]

149/4. EXT. PORCHWAY. ALLEY. NIGHT

[*We see* TOPLIS *in the shadows of the rear exit, still in the building.*

He opens the rear exit door – and is grabbed and thrown at the far wall of the alley by two policemen.

One policeman keeps him pinned against the wall.

The other man in the dim light from the back alley lamppost looks carefully at TOPLIS]

TOPLIS: *All right, all right!*

FELLOW SNOOP: It's not him.

[*The grip is loosened slightly on* TOPLIS]

POLICE SERGEANT: Well, who is it then?

TOPLIS: I'm the caretaker.

[*Looks aggrieved. As well as bloody mouthed*]

FELLOW SNOOP: Sorry about that – we just can't be too . . . who did that to you?

TOPLIS: Some bastard socialist – now what's going on?

FELLOW SNOOP: Police business.

[*The* FELLOW SNOOP *goes to the doorway*]

POLICE SERGEANT: And none of your business – so make sure it stays that way.

FELLOW SNOOP: Just take a walk, hey. A long one.

POLICE SERGEANT: Bournemouth and back. *Now.*

[TOPLIS *is released. He turns away meekly and walks down the alleyway. No pace. He turns towards the lights of the main street*]

150/4. EXT. ASSEMBLY HALL. NIGHT

[*We see* TOPLIS *turn into the street.*

We see the outside of the hall where notices announce a public meeting on behalf of the Labour Party.

The inevitable straggle of ex-servicemen with their medals pinned to their jackets, selling matches and bootlaces.

He crosses the road quickly and hides in a doorway.

There is a police van between TOPLIS *and the front entrance of the hall, parked in front of the taxi waiting for* STRANGE. *He has seen three men standing with their backs turned. Two are very big. One is very small.*

As TOPLIS *watches, the small man turns sideways to talk to one of the other men, whispers as the other man leans down.*

And TOPLIS *sees that it is* EDWIN WOODHALL.

He stays very still, in shock. Then his eyes look everywhere. Finally, he turns away.

As TOPLIS *does so, we hear a smattering of applause from those few who had waited for* STRANGE*'s entrance into the street.*

TOPLIS *turns again. Sees* STRANGE *coming out of the building with his four 'minders' around him.*

TOPLIS *moves sideways into the shop doorway, still watching. Opens his mouth to shout. Nothing comes out. He coughs, and tries again.*

As we see, at great speed, two of the so-called minders of STRANGE *virtually pick him up off his feet and hurtle him towards the police van.*

The three big men with WOODHALL *move forward and bar the way to any protestors, using force at the first opportunity.*

WOODHALL *turns and follows* STRANGE *and his escort.*

STRANGE *is pushed into the interior of the van.*

The two minders disappear into the street furtively.

WOODHALL *enters the van, a glint of a gun clearly in his hand. The van sets off down the road.*

TOPLIS *comes out of his hiding place, very carefully, and then slips away the way he has come – looking as though he has seen a ghost*]

151/4. INT. 'INTERVIEW' ROOM. NIGHT

[STRANGE *and* WOODHALL.

Two chairs. A desk, a notebook, a file in front of WOODHALL]

WOODHALL: . . . You were very . . . impressive at the . . . meeting.

STRANGE: So I've been told.

WOODHALL: Very noble. The references to war heroes. The cenotaph.

[*Looks down at his notes*]

'Comrades who died in vain'.

[*Looks up*]

In the war. A moving tribute. It's all going extremely well really, isn't it? Already there is considerable speculation that you're going to win.

STRANGE: That's up to the people who vote.

WOODHALL: . . . Not entirely. Fortunately.

STRANGE: Meaning?

WOODHALL: Oh . . . well, people can be influenced. Opinions can be changed.

[*Smiles*]

. . . Past events can be . . . recalled . . . revealed . . . Made public. So I'm afraid you are going to have to withdraw from this election. And disappear from public life.

[*Silence*]

That *is* a generous offer. I have been told to tell you that if you were to prove difficult about it, the alternatives would be far more . . . damaging . . . In all honesty, I do think my masters are being remarkably . . . decent.

[WOODHALL *takes a poster-size piece of paper from out of the file. Holds it up and turns it around to* STRANGE. *It is the wanted poster for* TOPLIS]

Tell me . . . have you seen him on your travels? During your . . . war years, perhaps?

[STRANGE *looks again at the poster, looks at* WOODHALL. *No flicker*]

STRANGE: How long have my two 'colleagues' been working for you?

WOODHALL: Since before they worked for you – it's a sad story, isn't it? But have you seen this man?

STRANGE: And who do you work for?

WOODHALL: Now come on, play the white man – I asked first.

STRANGE: Never seen him before in my life – *who do you work for?*

WOODHALL [*slowly*]: Liar . . . I am employed by the government.

STRANGE: Not the Tory Party?

[WOODHALL *smiles*]

And what if there was a Socialist Government?

WOODHALL: I don't deal in dreams.
STRANGE: No. Just in nightmares.

152/4. INT. ANNIE WEBSTER'S KITCHEN AND LIVING ROOM. DAY

[ANNIE *walking in from the kitchen with an envelope, towards* FRANK, *quietly dying at the fireplace*]

ANNIE: . . . It's registered.
FRANK: Who do we owe?
[ANNIE *opens the letter. Paper money slips out. She catches it*]
ANNIE: . . . Frank! . . .
[*Looks at a slip of paper. We leave her totally perplexed about the complexities of human nature. Particularly* PERCY TOPLIS*'s*]

153/4. EXT. DOROTHY'S HOUSE. DAY

[*We see* DOROTHY *at the door to her empty house, a suitcase in hand, holding her house keys.*
Then turning and walking towards another party of four suited men.
As she marches past them, she flicks the keys at them. Hard.
Inevitably, they are fumbled and dropped to the ground.
As she continues down the drive, she doesn't look back]

154/4. INT. WHITEHALL. ROOM. DAY

[*A dining room of some distinction.*
In some manner it should be quietly established that we are in Whitehall or in some such rooms of power.
The dining table, and the people around it, should be heaving with food and drink and rank and position.
But it is a relatively small gathering. Eight men, six in civilian clothing, two high-ranking Army officers.
The conversation is uncivilized but mellow.
At first only drinks are raised. We will hear snatches of conversation]

UNCIVILIZED: . . . bloody fool if you ask me, to himself and to his 'party' – I'm glad to say. That speech of his – I mean it beggars belief.

MELLOW: I read it, William, it made me laugh out loud – all that about 'heroes'. Some hero – A deserter, a mutineer and a socialist!

SERIOUS CIVILIAN: It's worth repeating, gentlemen, that what is happening now, the strikes, the increase in violent crimes, unionization and so on . . . has to be seen in the context of The War. The War has been a tragedy for us all but none more so than for the working classes – and without –

HIGH RANKING: Yes, yes, that's all well and good, Willy, but nevertheless, the likes of Strange and the others – that Top Fellow must be tracked down.

MELLOW: What 'Top Fellow' – I demand to know – have we got a Bolshevik in the Cabinet?

[*Some laughter*]

HIGH RANKING: Come on, Edwin, take the floor, take some praise, tell all. Go on, stand up, young man – not you Arthur, you're sixty-three – stand up and receive our generous th – oh I see, you already are standing up.

[*More laughter.* HIGH RANKING *smirks*]

I didn't mean to er . . .

[*Finally we see* WOODHALL. *Twenty-five years younger than everyone else around the table, flattered by being there, and willing to take any insult whatsoever. From any of them. He smiles happily*]

WOODHALL: That's quite all right, Sir George.

HIGH RANKING: Good. Good. Well, gentlemen.

[*They all begin to stand up. He stands, drink in hand*]

. . . and remember, Edwin, people like you are preserving the very fabric of decent society.

[*Looks around*]

The *Telegraph* said as much only this morning.

[*Nods*]

Er. Top . . .

WOODHALL: Toplis. Percy.

HIGH RANKING: Yes. That's the chap – I was at Woolwich with Andrew Thomson, you know, a fine man, a gentleman – I was glad to be a part of this exercise, I can tell you – but we'll get him – won't we, Edwin? 'Course we will. Good hunting.

[*We leave them as they raise their glasses to* EDWIN WOODHALL]

155/4. INT. COUNTRY HOTEL. BEDROOM. DAY

[*A hotel bedroom.*
TOPLIS *looking out of the window at the winter countryside.*
DOROTHY *joins him*]

DOROTHY: A long walk . . . ? A slow drive? A cold picnic?
TOPLIS: It could snow.
DOROTHY [*lightly*]: It could; it would be lovely if it did.
[TOPLIS *turns away from the window. Above all, he looks tired and drawn. He sits down, facing away from* DOROTHY *and the window*]
Cheer up . . . Johnny. This is the quietest you've been since I've known you. Come on, 'Mystery Man'. You always have a story – you always have an answer – different clothes – different names – different cars – you turned up on a push-bike one weekend.
TOPLIS: I couldn't get any petrol – Dorothy, please don't ask questions, I'll only tell you lies.
DOROTHY [*laughs*]: You think you own the copyright on lies?
[TOPLIS *leaves the window seat. He looks down towards* DOROTHY. *Shrugs*]
TOPLIS: On one or two of them.
DOROTHY: Not on mine.
TOPLIS: Don't.
[TOPLIS *sits on the bed*]
DOROTHY: Yes, yes. I will.
[DOROTHY *sits on the bed*]
What about my lies, Johnny? You know. You know your high society Nottingham lady, friend of the Duke of Portland, is not the lady she pretends to be. You know that. You played burglar in my empty house. And you still won't talk about it!
TOPLIS: I'll go now.
[*Starts to rise. She forces him down*]
DOROTHY: No, you just listen to me – listen, you dog –
[*He laughs in surprise*]
I don't want you going away again. I want you to stay with me. I want you to live with me – 'sometimes' isn't enough for me anymore – I want all the time. I want that boy that's there in you behind that . . . that thug's embrace. That –
TOPLIS: *That what?*
DOROTHY: Let me . . . I want to show you where I was born. And

why I chose this hotel. Johnny . . . Johnny . . . I was born in the next village.

TOPLIS: Geography has never really interested me, Dorothy.

DOROTHY: When you went to London, something happened. What was it – what's gone wrong?

TOPLIS: Do you think . . . Listen, when I came back from France – when I came back – and everything was the way it was – and worse – but that's how it is – that's how most people's lives are – that's how people's lives are made to be – miserable – desperate . . . but me – I thought, 'No, not me, they won't get me, because I don't care' . . . But what happens if you do care? I feel like an old man, I feel like a dead man on leave . . . Why do I feel like that at the age of twenty-one?

DOROTHY [*double takes*]: Tw – twenty-one?

[*She rises*]

Twenty-bloody-one? Oh my God!

TOPLIS: So I lied . . . Lies . . . Lies are . . . Lies are the only truth I know.

DOROTHY: Oh my God.

[DOROTHY *sits back on the bed*]

Good God – twenty-one – don't tell anyone else – if this gets out . . .

[*She starts to laugh, takes hold of him*]

TOPLIS: Are you listening to me?

DOROTHY: Yes. Yes. And I'm taking you out.

TOPLIS [*flatly*]: As long as you don't take me away . . .

[DOROTHY *embraces* TOPLIS *and kisses him*]

157/4. INT. CAR. DOROTHY'S VILLAGE. DAY

[TOPLIS *and* DOROTHY. *They are in a village of similar poverty to Blackwell, near a row of houses that are of a similar condition to* MRS TOPLIS*'s hovel.*

There is suspicion and sourness in the faces of those few watching. DOROTHY *stares out*]

TOPLIS: You lived there?

DOROTHY: Most of my life.

[*She looks towards him*]

You see, I was never worth a bean, Johnny. The man I married had more style and nerve and even less money than me. We were staying with the Duke of Portland, and he fell down the stairs in the dead of night and broke his neck. They said it was the drink and the darkness. But it wasn't.

TOPLIS: It was burglary.

DOROTHY: Yes.

158/4. EXT. COUNTRY LANE AND INT. CAR. DERBYSHIRE ROAD. DAY

[TOPLIS *and* DOROTHY *are driving along a road, which is narrow, going slowly downhill.*

TOPLIS *is talking like a man released from solitary*]

TOPLIS: I could have – when I first saw you – I thought 'aye-aye' – the car – the house – I thought I could use all that – I could do with your money.

DOROTHY: I didn't have any.

TOPLIS: I know. I know that now.

DOROTHY: Remember I saw an officer and a gentleman and a wit and a card. I thought you had money.

[*They both grin*]

TOPLIS: Ah well. But I couldn't let you keep me. That's why I was always away. Trying to keep myself, and you . . . And all that.

[*He stops, focuses on the road ahead. And we see four men walking in front of them. Three big men and one very small man, dressed like hikers. The small man is wearing a balaclava-type hat.* TOPLIS *lets his foot off the accelerator. The car stops. He turns around and sees a car with two men in it behind him. He turns wildly. She stares at him*]

DOROTHY: Press the horn.

TOPLIS: No . . . no.

[DOROTHY *sounds the horn.* TOPLIS *grabs hold of her arm. The men are walking close in front of them. They do not react.* TOPLIS *looks around again*]

Don't, don't – it's a trap.

[DOROTHY *doesn't understand*]

I'm sorry. I'm sorry.

[*One of the big men in front turns around. Grabs hold of one of the other men. He gesticulates. They all turn around – and wave in apology. We see that they are all deaf mutes. We go back to see* TOPLIS *virtually down on the floor of the car.* DOROTHY *looks down at him*]

DOROTHY: Unless you're wanted dead or alive by the deaf and dumb society, I'd get up off the floor . . .

[TOPLIS *slowly and suspiciously climbs up and looks towards the men in front of him. The car following* TOPLIS*'s overtakes. One is using sign language. 'What a dickhead!' The others start laughing as they look towards* TOPLIS]

TOPLIS: There's a few things you should know about me.

DOROTHY: And not before time . . .

159/4. EXT. ON A CLIFF HEAD. DAY

[*Walking along alone, we see* STRANGE. *Perhaps we are not aware that he is on a cliff head.*

He is wearing an overcoat. He walks on, reaches the very edge of the cliff. We now hear and see a raging winter's high tide beneath him. He takes a drink of whisky.

He walks off the edge of the cliff]

160/4. INT. CAR. COUNTRY ROAD. DAY

[TOPLIS *driving. Trying to break the land speed record.*]

DOROTHY [*points to the paper*]: It says here it was suicide. He'd been drinking heavily . . .

TOPLIS: That wasn't suicide. He wouldn't take anyone else's life – he isn't going to take his own. He loved . . . he cared.

[*Winces at the word*]

He was a decent man – I laughed at him for it – and they murdered him because of it.

DOROTHY: You don't know that, Johnny – and can we please drive on the road.

[*He slows down*]

TOPLIS: He arrested him. I've looked in the papers all week. Not a word. But Charles went in that van with him and he had a gun – they weren't going to the Savoy. Or the Ritz.

DOROTHY: Are you sure it was the same person?

TOPLIS [*nods his head*]: I saw his face. When he took the Stranger. It was him. He was there in France – he was after us then – and he still is – all three foot seven of him . . . And the problem is, my dear, I think it's me he really wants . . .

[*Irish*]

'You don't know the Mountains of Mourne, do you?'

[*As* DOROTHY *looks at him, he begins singing again, 'let the great big world keep turning'. As we fade*]

[*Sings*]: Let the great big world keep turning,
Never mind if I've got you,
For I only know that I want you so,
And there's no one else will do . . .

161/4. INT. PARKED CAR. NIGHT

[*The car is parked beside Stonehenge.*
TOPLIS *and* DOROTHY. *She has her arm around him.*
He is smoking a cigarette. As she completes the rest of the song]

DOROTHY [*sings*]: For I only know that I want you so,
And there's no one else will do.
You have simply set me yearning,
And for ever I'll be true,
Let the great big world keep on turning round
Now I've found someone like you . . .
How do you feel now?

TOPLIS: Cold.

[TOPLIS *hands his cigarette to* DOROTHY]

I'm all right.

DOROTHY: You've just seen too much, Johnny. All your generation saw too much.

TOPLIS: No . . . a lot of them didn't see enough . . . But I'm going back in . . .

[TOPLIS *turns to her and nods*]

No, I am, safety in numbers . . . and somehow I know where I am there . . . but out here –

[*Indicates the lights*]

– recently . . .

[*Shrugs*]

I'll sell the car, get a few bob and I'll come good.

[*Grins*]

Or bad.

[*He taps his fingers on the steering wheel. Holds them out in front of himself. Still still*]

I just can't get his face out of . . .

[*Touches his forehead*]

DOROTHY [*passionately*]: Of course you can't. Not yet, but you will. It must be like – you talked to me about ghosts a long time ago – when I was lying about my . . . husband – it's as if you've seen . . . a ghost.

TOPLIS: Or the future.

DOROTHY [*passionately and madly*]: No, Johnny! *No*! Come on, you cocky little – no, no, not little – my god, not little – you big boy. Big handsome warm generous filthy dirty don't care Johnny. Or Percy or Tom, Dick or Harry. And lover and son and *father*. Father, forgive me. For I know not what I do.

TOPLIS: Father?

DOROTHY: I think so . . . there, that'll take your mind off things . . .

162/4. INT. CAR. EXT. RECRUITING OFFICE SALISBURY. DAY

[TOPLIS *is in the driving seat.*

DOROTHY *at his side.*

The car is stationary. But the setting is not established]

TOPLIS [*quietly, flatly*]: She was a drunk and he was too, but he was a big soft drunk – and she had such a way of hurting him . . . I'd listen to her make him cry every night – and she made me cry too – and he'd plead with her to stop – and the more he asked the more he got. And every night when she started, it always ended with me – 'cos every night, according to her, I had a different father. Every man in the village was the father of me. Except that man.

DOROTHY: He'll know who his father is.

TOPLIS: Even if you have to tell him.

DOROTHY: *Don't.*

[DOROTHY *puts her hand over* TOPLIS*'s mouth. He kisses her*]

TOPLIS: This won't take long . . .

[TOPLIS *gets out of the car. We see him walk across the road and approach an Army recruiting office, to join a line of several men of some poverty*]

163/4. EXT/INT. NISSEN HUT. BULFORD CAMP, SALISBURY PLAIN. DAY

[*The Royal Army Service Corps' biggest base. 'It was a shambles. People were joining up in their thousands.*

And war veterans were trying to get out in their thousands. The rackets were enormous.'

We see two men, backs turned, but later to be recognized as TURNER *and* FALLOWS, *looking into a hut through a window*]

TURNER: It is, it's him! . . . Bloody hell, Harry . . .

[*We see* TOPLIS *in a Private's uniform, sitting on his bed in a hut, casually cleaning his boots. He glances up, and sees* TURNER *and* FALLOWS *move away from the window. He looks down, puzzled*]

164/4. INT. BAR IN A CAMP. NIGHT

[TOPLIS *enters a bar in the camp, crowded with soldiers.*

He approaches the bar, and orders. Another soldier, the rat-faced Private, HARRY FALLOWS, *sidles towards him*]

TOPLIS: A pint please.

[FALLOWS *puts his hand across*]

FALLOWS: I'll pay for this.

TOPLIS: No you won't.

[*Gives the money to the barman. Stares resolutely ahead. Silence.* FALLOWS *sneaks a look at* TOPLIS. *Who catches him*]

What are you looking at? Hey?

FALLOWS: I've got a message for you. Someone wants to meet you.

TOPLIS: Well you tell someone I'm here.

FALLOWS: He wants to meet you in private.

TOPLIS: Tell him I prefer public meetings. I also prefer drinking on my own.

[TOPLIS *pointedly turns his back slightly away from* FALLOWS *and starts to move away from the bar. Finally* FALLOWS *mumbles humbly and stays at the bar*]

FALLOWS: Sorry about that. No offence meant . . .

165/4. INT. TOPLIS' HUT. NIGHT

[*We see* TOPLIS *enter his hut, later that night. The hut is in darkness*]

TOPLIS: Christ.

[*We hear him curse as he looks for some light. He doesn't find it, but lights come on. All the beds are empty. Nobody about except* TURNER *sitting in the centre of a long table, a bottle of Johnny Walker whisky, two glasses in front of him.* FALLOWS *is at the light. He stays there.* TOPLIS *turns towards the door. Two big soldiers come to the doorway and close it.* TOPLIS *opens it again and comes face to face with the two soldiers. He closes it and moves into the room, approaching the table*]

Don't mind me, boys . . .

TURNER: But this is for you.

TOPLIS: No – it's all right, you have it.

TURNER: I know you.

TOPLIS: Fancy that – where's the rest of my hut?

TURNER: I sent them away, they'll be back later. But I know you.

TOPLIS: So?

TURNER: We've met before.

TOPLIS: Sorry, I've had such a varied life . . .

TURNER: I thought you might not recognize me. Not like this. Not like I am now.

[TOPLIS *is getting closer and more confident*]

TOPLIS: Ah, I see. You were someone different at the time. Perhaps we met in another life. Who knows, perhaps you were Napoleon and I was Wellington, yes, it's coming back to me now, there we were at Waterloo – the train was late . . . Stop pissing about.

TURNER [*grins at* FALLOWS]: You might remember me more like this.

[*He leans down and takes a tank driver's chain mail mask off the bed. He briefly puts it on, or up to his face*]

I kept it as a souvenir of that day in Etaples.

TOPLIS: I *was* right. It was another life . . .

TURNER: Come on, Percy. You're with friends.

TOPLIS: Now you've really got me worried.

TURNER: Look, we all know, but it's all right – you were a hero, that day.

TOPLIS: *No I wasn't.* A hero.

TURNER: Relax – you're with me. I'm Tommy Turner – I run

everything here. Everything worth running, if you follow my meaning. Just tell me what you want – I'll arrange it. If it's mine to give you, Percy, you can have it.

TOPLIS: . . . I want you to forget Percy Toplis for a start. I signed up as Johnny Walker, and that's my name.

[TURNER *lifts up the 'Johnny Walker' bottle and pours a drink*]

TURNER: I'll drink to that.

[*Laughter from* TURNER *and* FALLOWS]

TOPLIS: I want a gun.

FALLOWS: I've got one. You can have mine.

TOPLIS: I want my own. A good one.

[*Shrugs*]

A Webley Six.

TURNER: You'll have it tonight.

TOPLIS: And I want to make a lot of money. *Fast.*

[TURNER *looks around at* FALLOWS, *who has sneaked forward.* TURNER *grins*]

TURNER: A lot of money fast. You see, I told you you'd like him.

[*Back to* TOPLIS]

Know anything about petrol, Percy – Johnny?

TOPLIS: Yeah, it makes motor cars go. And I drank a lot of it in France.

TURNER: You're going to know a lot more about it tomorrow . . .

166/4. INT. TOPLIS'S HUT. NIGHT

[TOPLIS *is in bed, later that night.*

FALLOWS *comes to the side of the bed, with a wrapped-up gun. Then crouches on the floor by him. Looks at* TOPLIS]

TOPLIS: Can I have *Goldilocks and the Three Bears?*

[FALLOWS *slips the gun to* TOPLIS]

FALLOWS: It's a good gun.

TOPLIS: . . . Is it?

FALLOWS: Aren't you going to look at it?

TOPLIS: No.

FALLOWS: . . . What do you want it for?

TOPLIS: To kill people that keep me awake at night.

FALLOWS [*laughs*]: Don't be like that. What was it like over there? I was too young to go, see. What was it like, killing someone? You know, really killing them face to face?

TOPLIS: I wouldn't know.

FALLOWS: Oh go on, Percy –

TOPLIS: *My name's Johnny.*

FALLOWS: I wish I'd been there with you. You're famous – you are – even before you came here I'd heard Tommy Turner talk about you. You sat in that General's car, didn't you? You on your own with him. Bloody hell! And here I am now, me and Percy Toplis.

[TOPLIS *takes his hand out from beneath the bedclothes and pulls* FALLOWS *furiously and fast towards him by his tunic*]

TOPLIS: I shall break the habit of a lifetime and murder you if you don't go away right now.

SLEEPING SOLDIER: Bloody shut up.

TOPLIS: And if you mention 'Percy Toplis' once more I'll tear you so far apart they'll bury you in five different cemeteries.

[FALLOWS *laughs as* TOPLIS *releases him*]

FALLOWS: You're a case, you are, it's all right, I'll go now, no offence meant . . .

[*He goes.* TOPLIS *stares after him in near disbelief*]

167/4. EXT. PETROL DEPOT. BULFORD THE NEXT DAY

[TURNER, FALLOWS *and* TOPLIS *near the petrol tanks.*

We see a soldier with a black moustache, standing by a lorry, as it is filled up. He looks up and winks towards them]

TURNER: Another . . . 'full tank', Johnny . . .

TOPLIS: Remarkable, Tommy, so what do you need me for?

TURNER: Distribution, Johnny. Haulage firms, bus services, taxi companies, all crying out for cut-price petrol, and this little racket isn't little anymore.

[*Puts his arm around* TOPLIS]

Needs someone like you to add your considerable charm and organization to the proceedings.

TOPLIS: And what do I get out of it?

TURNER: The same as me. Straight down the middle with everything you handle. Once we've made our donations and deductions to unworthy causes such as Harry here.

TOPLIS: Forgive my suspicions, it's just I'm not used to such generosity . . .

TURNER: Call it for old times' sake as well.

[*The question* TURNER *has been dying to ask*]

You do remember me there, don't you?

TOPLIS: Totally. Totally, Tommy – to be honest, the minute I saw you – it's me, y'see, I don't like to . . be recognized.

TURNER: Sure, sure.

[*They have walked on. We see them by a parked civilian motorcar*]

This is yours for the duration, Johnny. Now, you've got a meeting at eight with the taxi driver who's one of my contacts here –

FALLOWS: Sydney Spencer.

TURNER: Who's asking you?

[*To* TOPLIS]

He's the local hard-case and big mouth – if you can cope with him, you can cope with anything.

[*Takes an envelope from his pocket as he talks*]

Harry'll be there – and here's your pass and a few quid for drinks. Anything else you want?

[TOPLIS *grins*]

169/4. INT. CAR. COUNTRY COTTAGE. DAY

[TOPLIS *and* DOROTHY *draw up in car. He is in officers uniform.* DOROTHY *and then* TOPLIS, *get out, outside a* Country Life *cottage with a 'for sale or rent' sign*]

DOROTHY: Are you . . .

[*Flatly*]

. . . crazy?

TOPLIS [*shakes his head*]: I've fallen on my feet, Dorothy . . . we both have. Just go into the estate agent this afternoon, tell them you want to rent it with a view to purchase.

[*Looks at her*]

Use your very best high society Duke of Portland voice.

DOROTHY [*deep and bass*]: 'My good man, come here a moment, would you.'

TOPLIS: Duchess then.

[*They start laughing, and laughing. And laughing, they kiss*]

170/4. INT. BAR. ANOTHER PUBLIC HOUSE

[TOPLIS, FALLOWS, *and the gross heavyweight* SYDNEY SPENCER *are present.*
TOPLIS *is dressed as a Captain*]

SPENCER: It's too dear.
TOPLIS [*easily*]: Then fill up at a petrol pump.
SPENCER: It's too dear for the chances I take.
TOPLIS: We think we sell it too cheap for the chances we take. Now surely . . .
SPENCER: And not only that, I've been sold short the last three times, ten gallons a time, that's all, but that's not the point. *Is it?*
TOPLIS [*warmly*]: Can you prove it, Mr Spencer?
SPENCER: I could probably convince the proper authorities . . .
TOPLIS: Now, there'd be nothing gained by that, would there – another pint of bitter, is it?
SPENCER: Amazing what one little telephone call could do. And don't soft soap me – just don't let it happen again.
[TOPLIS *trying for charm and trying too hard*]
TOPLIS: I have been brought in, Mr Spencer, for exactly the kind of problem you describe. You see me, you deal with me – and you'll be a satisfied man.
SPENCER: I'm acting for others, you know – I've only got the three taxis – there's over twenty lads I'm representing. Any shortages – it's one of my cabs goes off the road.
TOPLIS: Hah, I could see you were a man of principle – and we're making a note of all this – *aren't we, Harry?*
[FALLOWS *struggles for a pencil and a piece of paper out of his tunic*]
Thirty gallons is thirty gallons –
SPENCER: And a pint's a pint.
[*Spins the glass towards* TOPLIS]
They serve food in here, you know.

171/4. INT. TOPLIS'S HUT. DAY

[TOPLIS *is lying on his bed, boots off, reading a newspaper, drinking tea. The hut is empty.*
FALLOWS *comes in*]

FALLOWS: You've had a visitor.

TOPLIS: *What?*

FALLOWS: A visitor. Someone was looking for you but he's gone now . . .

[FALLOWS *sits on the bed.* TOPLIS *sits up.*]

TOPLIS: What was he like – *was he small?*

FALLOWS: Anything but – it's your friend and mine, Sydney Spencer.

TOPLIS: Why didn't you say so – for crying out loud.

FALLOWS: No offence meant. Anyway, he wants to see you tonight. Usual place. Tommy says I should be there.

TOPLIS: All right – but listen! If anyone small ever comes around here – really small, funny-looking sod, wavy hair but above all – small – you don't know me – *right?*

[TOPLIS *goes back to his newspaper*]

FALLOWS: Right. I won't forget that, Johnny. Very small, wavy hair . . . Tommy took a gun with him every time he went to see Spencer . . . you need to with Spencer . . . he hit me once, Spencer did, broke two of my teeth – there at the back – I thought Tommy was going to pull his gun on him . . . but he didn't in the end . . . I've got the same gun as you, you know, Webley Mark Six . . .

[TOPLIS *ignores him*]

I thought what's good enough for you is good enough for me . . . Shall I come with you then? Tommy says I should come with you.

[TOPLIS *says nothing*]

I'd take your gun if I was you . . .

172/4. INT. PARKED TAXI. NIGHT

[*We see* TOPLIS, SPENCER *and* FALLOWS *in* SPENCER*'s taxi.*

SPENCER *is shouting the odds about something that we cannot quite hear.*

TOPLIS *is doing his best to remain calm and patient.*

FALLOWS *is sitting in the back seat, silent.*

During this we hear the voice of TOMMY TURNER]

TURNER [V.O.]: Now he'll deny this, 'cos that's the sort of feller he is. But I'm not kidding – he took the handkerchief away from his face, cool as a cucumber, right, the General standing there in full dress, right, and he said, 'You're a broken man, Thomson, and I've broken you. Now sign that before I put a bullet through what passes for your brains.'

173/4. INT. PRIVATE ROOM. MESS. NIGHT

[*A private room in the mess at Bulford Camp.*

The ring leaders are around a table, drinking. They include the soldier with the moustache, and TOMMY TURNER. *Someone 'guards' the door.*

TURNER *is talking*]

TURNER: . . . He would have done an' all, you know, but the silence in the room . . . you should have heard it. And then – and then –

[TOPLIS *knocks on the door. The guard opens it a touch then lets* TOPLIS *and* FALLOWS *in.* TOPLIS *approaches the table, as they all look at him*]

I was just . . . telling the lads here a little bit about Etaples –

[TURNER *passes* TOPLIS *an envelope*]

I know you don't like saying much, but there's no problems with us, I can guarantee you that.

TOPLIS: I know. It's the others. It's always the others.

TURNER: – Come on, 'Johnny', sit down, have a drink, swop some stories, everyone's been dying to have a chat with you . . .

[*To group*]

Like I was saying. If anyone can handle Spencer it's our 'Johnny'.

[TOPLIS *sits down reluctantly*]

174/175/4. INT. TOPLIS'S COTTAGE LOUNGE NIGHT

[*We see* TOPLIS *and* DOROTHY *in the lounge of their rented cottage.*

DOROTHY *is in nightclothes, on the sofa, with a blanket and a book; she has been waiting again*]

TOPLIS: There's always a price, Dorothy. Even the things you steal aren't free.

[TOPLIS *hands an envelope to* DOROTHY. DOROTHY *quickly counts the money*]

DOROTHY: If you keep making this money . . .

TOPLIS: That's what keeps me going.

[TOPLIS *moves round to sit beside* DOROTHY]

See out the rest of the winter, get through the spring and summer . . .

[DOROTHY *sits up to make room for* TOPLIS]

. . . have the baby . . . and then . . .

DOROTHY: A one-way ticket.

TOPLIS: For three.

DOROTHY: First class.

TOPLIS: But of course.

[*They kiss*]

176/4. EXT. CAR PARK, BULFORD PUB. NIGHT

[*We see* TOPLIS *and* FALLOWS *waiting, as headlights approach*]

FALLOWS: What do I have to do to prove myself to you?

TOPLIS: Emigrate. Now when we get in, you get in the back and don't say a word.

FALLOWS: Anything you say, Johnny.

[*The taxi stops.* TOPLIS *and* FALLOWS *are in the headlights. A man and a woman get out of the taxi, crossing the car park to the pub; they look at* TOPLIS. TOPLIS *turns his back,* FALLOWS *doesn't. They get into the car*]

177/4. INT. TAXI. COUNTRY ROAD. NIGHT

[*We see* SPENCER *driving his taxi, through the countryside.*
TOPLIS *is in the front, at the side of him.*
FALLOWS *is in the back, directly behind* TOPLIS]

SPENCER: You're making a bloody fortune out of me.

TOPLIS: And I suppose you're starving.

[*Evenly*]

Look, it's three and six a gallon at the pump, Sydney, you're getting it for two bob. Although at the moment you're getting it for bugger all.

SPENCER: I've got the money

[*Taps his wallet pocket*]

and you'll be paid – when the price is right.

TOPLIS: That is the price – and there's nothing wrong with it.

SPENCER: One and sixpence.

TOPLIS: I'd rather set fire to it first.

[*Pause*]

FALLOWS [*suddenly*]: It's really lonely round here, isn't it . . .

SPENCER: What's that got to do with anything?

FALLOWS: Nothing. Just nothing. No offence meant . . . Just . . . lonely.

SPENCER [*to* TOPLIS]: You'd get five years for this, you know . . . if you were caught. Five years. Minimum.

TOPLIS: You're wrong, Sydney. I wouldn't get five years – and I'm not going to get caught.

SPENCER: Take one and six then – twelve hundred gallons – still ninety pounds.

[*Smirks as he finally looks at* TOPLIS]

I worked it out.

TOPLIS: You wasted your time . . . By the way, I think it's a pretty lousy trick selling it to the other taxi drivers for two and ninepence.

[SPENCER *grabs hold of* TOPLIS *by his jacket as he drives on*]

SPENCER: Don't get clever with me, Walker, or else it'll be one and threepence.

[SPENCER *throws* TOPLIS *against the passenger door violently. We see* TOPLIS *put his hand towards his pocket as though reaching for a gun, and if looks could kill*]

I'm charging you for this journey as well, y'know.

[*Looks down at his mileage*]

Already near a quid!

[*We watch* TOPLIS, *his face a mixture of malice and hesitancy. Until*]

TOPLIS [*putting his head down*]: One and six then.

[SPENCER *laughs*]

Pull up and pay us and let's get it over with.

[SPENCER *pulls in to the side of the road.* TOPLIS *looks away.* SPENCER *turns and grins hugely at him.* SPENCER *takes his wallet out of his inside pocket, grins at* TOPLIS]

SPENCER: You did say a shilling, didn't you?

[TOPLIS *stares bleakly at* SPENCER. *We hear a gun being cocked. We hear a voice from the back of the taxi*]

FALLOWS: Just give us the wallet.

[*We see* FALLOWS *with a gun in his hand, pointing it very near to* SPENCER*'s head*]

I've got a gun – now give my friend your wallet. Or else.

[*We see* TOPLIS *putting his hands over his face in disbelief*]

TOPLIS [*to himself*]: Oh Jesus Christ.

SPENCER [*laughs*]: Sod off, you little worm.

[TOPLIS *puts his hand on the catch to open the taxi door.* SPENCER *grabs at the gun barrel, holds it – and* FALLOWS *shoots* SPENCER. *The blood spatters onto* FALLOWS, *who screams; onto* TOPLIS, *who cringes in the seat.* SPENCER *slumps onto the driving wheel*]

178/4. EXT. ROADSIDE. NIGHT

[*We see* TOPLIS *dragging, with difficulty, the body of* SPENCER *towards a hedge, about forty yards off the roadway.*

We can still see SPENCER*'s car on the road. And we can hear* FALLOWS *sobbing and near yelping from inside the car.* TOPLIS *runs back to the taxi and gets in*]

179/4. INT. PARKED TAXI. NIGHT

[TOPLIS *takes* FALLOWS*'s gun from his lap.*

We see TOPLIS *sitting on the driver's seat. Kneeling towards* FALLOWS. *He now has a gun in his hand, pointing it at* FALLOWS *for some time.* FALLOWS *goes into more hysterics*]

TOPLIS [*after an eternity*]: You've killed somebody. It's not like in the comics, is it, Harry?

FALLOWS [*blubbering*]: I thought . . . I thought you wanted me to do it –

[TOPLIS *holds up* SPENCER*'s wallet*]

TOPLIS: *You what* – for ninety pounds and some loose change – Jesus! *Jesus!*

[TOPLIS *raises the gun as if to hit him*]

FALLOWS: I thought you'd be – I did it for you, Percy.

TOPLIS: You should have killed yourself then – and I wish I could kill you – I wish you'd try and kill me.
FALLOWS: I wouldn't – I wouldn't do that.
TOPLIS: . . . You already have.

180/4. INT. TAXI. COUNTRY ROAD. NIGHT

[*We see them travelling along the road, very fast.*

We see TOPLIS *clenched and smoking;* FALLOWS *wide-eyed and trembling in the back of the car*]

TOPLIS: I can't believe – you little arsehole – an hour before – what happens – there's two people in this taxi – and where are we? – we're standing there in the headlights – we may as well have been carrying placards with our names on.
FALLOWS: I've never done anything like this before –
ROPLIS [*turns around*]: *Shut up, shut up, shut up!*
FALLOWS: . . . I want to go to the toilet . . .
TOPLIS: Piss in the car, I don't care, piss on his blood, go on, you've pissed on his life.

[*Turns*]

You . . . *you* . . . you –

[TOPLIS *turns back to the road. Swerves to avoid running off it and the car runs into a ditch.* FALLOWS *runs out of the car and away off the road into the darkness of the surrounding fields.* TOPLIS *gets out of the car, grabs his gun, and fires blindly into the darkness. Emptying the gun into nowhere finally. And at nothing. The last shot goes into the ground at his feet*]

181/4. INT. TOPLIS'S COTTAGE. DAWN

[TOPLIS *at home, in civilian clothes, finishing packing in a hurry.*

He enters from the hall, puts down the suitcase and fetches his shaving things from kitchen]

DOROTHY: Johnny

[*In hallway*]

Johnny.

[*At kitchen doorway*]

TOPLIS: What's the point of talking about it?

[TOPLIS *puts shaving things in suitcase and monocle from mantel-piece*]

DOROTHY: But if you'd stayed the same – it's my fault – if you hadn't have met me – if we hadn't have come here – needed the money so much –

[TOPLIS *puts his hands on* DOROTHY]

TOPLIS: No, no. *No*, that is *not true*. It had to happen one day. Remember – a dead man on leave . . .

[*They hold one another*]

DOROTHY [*not flatly*]: No! . . . No!

TOPLIS: *Don't ever forget* if I hadn't have met you – I'd have been dead all my life – dead handsome –

[*Tries to smile*]

Dead clever – dead smart – but dead, and I wouldn't have missed being with you . . . for anything.

[*He goes into the hall and upstairs.* DOROTHY *follows*]

DOROTHY: I'm coming with you.

TOPLIS: No, you're not.

182/4. EXT. TOPLIS'S COTTAGE. DAWN

[*We see them as they leave the house. Dawn is breaking.*

DOROTHY *has a suitcase. She looks what she is – five months pregnant. She struggles after* TOPLIS *as he reaches the car*]

TOPLIS: You're not going to be there, Dorothy. Neither of you are.

[*He gets in the car. She gets in defiantly, puts the suitcase in the back*]

Get out of the car.

[*No answer. A long pause*]

Get out of the car . . .

[*Gently*]

Get out . . . pick me some flowers.

DOROTHY: I don't want to give you flowers.

TOPLIS: Just one then. No bouquets . . .

[*Smiles*]

Just one flower for Johnny.

[*Finally* DOROTHY *gets out. But just stands there. And even more finally, she opens the door and takes her suitcase out. They look at each other. He drives off*]

DOROTHY: . . . No flowers for Johnny.

[*A few yards on, he throws* SPENCER*'s wallet out of the window. It lands in the grass. He drives away down the lane*]

183/4. INT. INTERVIEW ROOM. DAY

[FALLOWS, *with two policemen – talking, and shaking*]

FALLOWS: He shot him. Then he tried to shoot me. He's killed lots of people. He's wanted by the Secret Service, Toplis. *Toplis*. You check up – he's wanted – he's a real killer . . . I'm lucky to be alive . . .

[*We leave them as he looks around anxiously*]

184/4. EXT/INT. WOODHALL'S HOUSE

[*Sunday afternoon.*

A garden. A small child fishing.

WOODHALL *and son playing. He is a wonderful father.*

The telephone rings.

WOODHALL *walks through into the house. His son gets to the telephone first.*

WOODHALL *sits down, his son sits in his lap. He answers the telephone, listens, then puts the receiver down, and puts his arm around the boy.*

He smiles happily]

185/4. MONTAGE. THE HUE AND CRY

185

[TOPLIS, *dressed as a civilian, is in the countryside walking, with a suitcase. Eating as he goes. He is unshaven, haunted*]

185(a)

[*A policeman cycles up to a clearing and goes to inspect a camouflaged object, removing branches to reveal* TOPLIS*'s abandoned car. On the* *windscreen, the* News of the World *with* TOPLIS*'s photograph dressed as a Captain, the headline 'the most wanted man in Britain'.*

Beside the headline scrawled in TOPLIS*'s handwriting 'I didn't do it'*]

185(b)

[FALLOWS *with police in police station, handcuffs being removed. He rubs his wrists and looks knowingly at the little man watching him –* WOODHALL]

185(c)

[*Police storming* TOPLIS*'s* MOTHER*'s house, breaking in as she sits, blind and terrified, by her dead fire. They break through the back door and go upstairs*]

185(d)

[*Newspaper headlines 'inquest finds* TOPLIS *guilty in absence' 'legal history made'. The newspaper is screwed up by* TOPLIS.

We see TOPLIS *sitting in the back of an empty coal truck. The truck moves off*]

185(e)

[*A policeman at his map adds another pin to those dotted around England, Scotland and Wales.*

We find a newspaper with headlines about dozens of sightings of TOPLIS *and then the man reading it – again* WOODHALL]

185(f)

[TOPLIS *asleep in a barn or outbuilding, covered in straw and newspapers*]

185(g)

[TOPLIS *leaving the Army Camp in Carlisle. Coming out of the cookhouse armed with food, and dressed as an RE Corporal.*

The soldiers watch him go. In awe.

He walks away between some huts and out of sight]

186/4. EXT/INT. SHOOTING LODGE. DAY

[*1 June, 1920. Early evening.*
Banffshire Highlands, Scotland.
The exterior of the Lecht Shooting Lodge. A bicycle is propped against the timbered wall, smoke is coming from the chimney.
A gamekeeper some distance away is watching the smoke. Then walks hurriedly away.
As we enter the interior of the Lodge we see a drawn, dirty-looking and tired TOPLIS. *He smashes the furniture for the fire. He is smashing up items such as three George II walnut armchairs and a Louis XVI giltwood writing table.*
A couple of dead rabbits are by the fire]

187/4. EXT/INT. SHOOTING LODGE. NIGHT

[*We see, in darkness,* JOHN GRANT, *the farmer,* JOHN MACKENSIE, *the Laird's gamekeeper, and 'the only policeman for this entire highland area', Constable* GEORGE GREIG. *They have shotguns and lanterns.*
We see them trying the door to the Shooting Lodge, which is locked. The GAMEKEEPER *has a key – but first they look through the windows*]

GAMEKEEPER [in shock]: As quietly as you can lads. It's all right. He's asleep . . . The furniture. He's burned the furniture.
[*The policeman takes his key, quietly opens the door. The three men charge into the room, guns ready. Candles flicker near to a huddle of blankets and the shape of a man. The three men surround it. All it is is blankets. They hear a voice behind them, near the door*]

TOPLIS: Don't turn around – and no messing about, because I don't care.
[*The* GAMEKEEPER *turns, gun in hand and brings his gun up to fire. We see* TOPLIS, *a trilby down, shadowing his eyes, as he fires his gun. We see the* GAMEKEEPER *shot in the chest. We see the* POLICEMAN *turning, gun raised. We see him shot, and falling on the candles. The lights go out. Two of the men are groaning.* TOPLIS *turns and runs from the cabin. We see him with the bike running down a track*]
Goodbye-ee,
Goodbye-ee,
Wipe the tear,

Baby dear,
From your eye-ee . . .

188/4. EXT. BORDER COUNTRY ROAD

1

[*The Scottish border.*
A vicar in his car is stopping for TOPLIS, *who is wearing a monocle. He speaks through the open window*]

TOPLIS: South. Anywhere south.
[*As the car leaves the scene, we see a bicycle with punctured tyres thrown into a stream*]

189/4. EXT. FULTON'S HOUSE. DAY

[*We see* TOPLIS *tramping along the road, dressed as before, but rougher still. Looking exhausted and unshaven, he approaches a small cottage. A plump middle-aged woman is working in her garden.*
TOPLIS *stops*]

TOPLIS: Excuse me, ma'am, I'm a bit down on my . . . you haven't got a cup of tea, have you? Please.
[*The woman goes to answer him, and looks at him to the point of a stare. She points into the house, hurries away to the window*]
MRS FULTON: Alf. Hey, Alf.
[TOPLIS *follows her hurried walk with his eyes for a second or two.* FULTON *wearing his police uniform leans out of the window*]
FULTON: Can I help?
[TOPLIS *starts running away towards some woods*]

190/4. INT. POLICE CONSTABLE AND MRS FULTON'S HOUSE

[MRS FULTON *looks in at the window.* FULTON *looks, sees* TOPLIS *running, then feverishly ransacks his 'wanted' notices in the table drawer. He finds the 'wanted' notice for* TOPLIS]

FULTON: That's him. *It's Toplis!*

191/4. EXT. WOODS NEARBY. DAY

[*We see* FULTON *walking through the woods, dodging trees, and calling, truncheon out*]

FULTON: . . . Hello . . . Coo-ee, are you there . . . hello . . .
[*As he is almost in front of a tree,* TOPLIS *steps from behind it, gun in hand, pointing at* FULTON*'s head.* FULTON *hides his truncheon behind his back and drops it*]
TOPLIS: Yes?
FULTON: . . . You haven't seen my wife, have you? I was looking . . .
[*He looks desperately to his side*]
Coo-ee, Mary! Mary . . .
[TOPLIS *breaks into a grin. Then starts to laugh. Wildly*]
TOPLIS: Well, that's the best yet.
[TOPLIS *moves a pace or two closer to* FULTON]
Oh look, there she is over there!
[TOPLIS *points.* FULTON *actually looks, and* TOPLIS *hits him over the head with his pistol.* FULTON *slumps to the ground.* TOPLIS *turns and runs away. Some distance on he shouts*]
Coo-ee Mary, are you there? Coo-ee Mary!

192/4. EXT. PENRITH ROAD. DAY

[FULTON *on his motorbike. 'In disguise': goggles, cap, tweed jacket and knickerbockers – with a bandage around his head.*
We see him on the Penrith road, suddenly increasing his speed and putting his head down and to one side.
We see him giving a wide berth on the road to a soldier walking]

TOPLIS: Mary. Coo-ee Mary.

193/4. INT. PENRITH POLICE STATION. DAY

[*We see pandemonium at Penrith Police Station as several policemen change out of their uniforms into civilian clothes. As* FULTON *loads a gun,* INSPECTOR RICHIE *is on the telephone, while trying to take his own jacket off*]

194/4. INT. CHIEF CONSTABLE'S LOUNGE

[*We see the lounge of the Chief Constable of Cumberland,* DE COURCY PARRY. *He is on the telephone, his son, Norman, nearby*]

DE COURCY PARRY: . . . Scotland Yard . . . Ah yes, my name is De Courcy Parry, Chief Constable of Cumberland . . . I know it's Sunday – but this is with regard to Percy Toplis . . . thank you.
[*To his son*]
Pull the map down, would you, Norman . . .
[NORMAN *pulls down the map*]
Hello.

195/4. EXT. WOODLANDS. DAY

[*Two teenage girls peeping through trees, giggling.*

They are watching a young man, TOPLIS, *washing himself at a stream in woodlands known as Thiefside, on the edge of the Penrith road.*

When he starts to change out of Army uniform into civilian clothing, they run off shrieking]

196/197/4. INT. CHIEF CONSTABLE'S LOUNGE DAY

[DE COURCY PARRY *on the telephone, his son* NORMAN *by the bureau, all ears*]

DE COURCY PARRY: . . . Well, let's hope it won't come to that . . . to be perfectly honest I don't know exactly how many guns we can get. But we'll do our best . . . Of course . . . goodbye.
[DE COURCY PARRY *puts down the telephone*]
[*to* NORMAN]: This Toplis character must be something very special . . . They're sending up a Secret Service chappie.
NORMAN: I'm sure I can be of *some* assistance, Father.
[DE COURCY PARRY looks at some papers]
DE COURCY PARRY: Well, I suppose you could go up to Alston and organize a road block.
NORMAN: That's miles away. He won't reach there.

[FATHER *looks at* NORMAN *severely*]

Oh very well then.

[*When* NORMAN*'s father turns back to answer the telephone, the son removes a Belgian automatic gun from the desk*]

DE COURCY PARRY: Hello. Yes. Parry here. Hello, hello, Inspector Ritchie. Every gun you can find, Ritchie – and every man . . . well if you need cars, commandeer them!

198/4. EXT. CROWN HOTEL. VILLAGE STREET AND BRIDGE. DAY

[*The barman,* EDWARD SPRUCE, *is being hustled out of the hotel by three men in mufti.*

We see an already-nervous SPRUCE *getting into a maroon, open, four-seater Armstrong motor car, alongside* FULTON, RITCHIE *and* BERTRAM.

The car draws away, as a ten-horsepower 1,000 cc American motor-cycle screams to a halt.

NORMAN DE COURCY PARRY *has arrived*]

NORMAN: *Stop, stop.*

RITCHIE: Pull over.

NORMAN: My father said to come and join you, chaps . . .

RITCHIE: Are you sure?

NORMAN: Yes.

RITCHIE: Well, come on then.

[*The car and motor cycle draw off and drive in convoy over a bridge*]

199/4. EXT. ROAD NORTH. DAY

['And so this strangest of all police convoys, followed by a goggled, leather-helmeted civilian motor-cyclist, moved north on to the Carlisle highway, the car driven by barman Spruce doing a steady 45 mph, with Fulton in the front passenger seat and the gun-carrying Ritchie and Bertram standing on either running board, clinging to the sides, capped, mufflered and raincoated.

Just north of the crossroads village of Plumpton, four miles from Penrith, the motley crew of apparent joy-riders passed a neat, unshaven, trilby hatted, suited young man carrying a brown paper parcel. They were nearly a mile past their target before the fact dawned on Fulton. He shouted up to Ritchie, who was grimly holding on to the inside of Spruce's front driver seat.']

FULTON: I'm sorry sir, but it's just struck me – I think we've just passed him . . .
RITCHIE [*having to roar*]: Turn around! Stop! Turn around!
[*We see the nerves all over* SPRUCE]

200/4. EXT. ROAD. SOUTH. DAY

[*We see* TOPLIS *walking along, as described, head down, stone-faced, as he hears a high-powered motor bike stop. He looks up.*

And sees NORMAN DE COURCY PARRY *some distance away, climbing off his bike. As he inspects it,* TOPLIS *can see him peering through the bike's framework as he walks.*

And as he hears a motor car approaching him from the rear]

TOPLIS [*to himself*]: Come on, come on, this time, this time little man, this time.
[TOPLIS *stops as he reaches the motorbike and watches as the car approaches. And* DE COURCY PARRY *stands up giving a thumbs-up sign. We join the car as it nears* TOPLIS]
RITCHIE: Now slower, Ted, slower and get nearer to him.
['Instead the car gathered speed and veered away from Toplis and past him for the second time']
For Christ's sake, Ted! What the hell's the matter with you!
['But the barman was too terrified to hear Ritchie, and with cloth cap pulled well down over a chalk white face, he took a firmer grip on the steering wheel and started heading back towards Penrith at a maximum 50 mph.'

As the car rocks dangerously from side to side, threatening to dislodge RITCHIE *and* BERTRAM, FULTON *grabs* SPRUCE *by the lapel of his coat to try to make him stop*]
FULTON: Stop, stop. Go back, Ted. I'm ordering you.
SPRUCE: The only orders I take are behind the bar.
[*He finishes up high pitched.* RITCHIE*'s gun pointed at him finally convinces him – in a fashion*]
Oh God, I'm going to die . . .
[*He pushes himself so far down in the seat that he can barely see over the instrument panel.* FULTON *has to help him steer*]

RITCHIE: Come on, come on. Hurry up and the minute anyone sees a gun, open fire . . .

[SPRUCE *drives the car into the verge and* RITCHIE *and* BERTRAM *jump off the running board. In the meantime,* TOPLIS *has approached* DE COURCY PARRY]

TOPLIS: Coo-ee Mary!

[DE COURCY PARRY *looks up at him, bewildered.*]

Who are those men that keep passing?

NORMAN: I er think they're . . . they're just out for a joy-ride.

TOPLIS: Then why did – do you know anyone small – do you?

NORMAN: What – I mean, how small?

TOPLIS: You gave them the thumbs up.

[*A gun can be seen in his pocket, his hand trembling near it*]

What did you do that for?

NORMAN: Well . . . I know two of them, and . . . my bike's broken down. I thought they may be able to help.

[*We hear the noise of the motor car's return in the distance*]

RITCHIE: Come on, come on.

[TOPLIS *turns to watch its approach.* DE COURCY PARRY *is shaking as well, moving his hand towards his own gun*]

TOPLIS: Here it comes . . . everything comes . . . and everything . . . you're never ready for it though, are you? The funny thing is . . . when I had nothing to lose, I always won . . . he looks small . . .

[*We can see the car approaching, a driver barely visible, two men hanging onto the side, hands on their guns.* TOPLIS *watches them come closer and closer, hand on gun in pocket, sad and resigned, near to mad laughter and tears. Closer and closer. The car arrives. He takes his gun out.* DE COURCY PARRY *takes his gun out. The driver peeps over the windscreen, looks at a gun, whines and faints. And* TOPLIS *does not open fire. But* FULTON, RITCHIE, BERTRAM *and* DE COURCY PARRY *do*]

RITCHIE: Got him!

SPRUCE: Oh God!

[TOPLIS *gets shot in the chest. His body shudders forward, trapping his tongue between his teeth. And* FULTON, RITCHIE *and* DE COURCY PARRY *are stunned and sickened.* SPRUCE *wakens from his faint and looks out. Faints again*]

201/4. INT. WEIGHTS AND MEASURES ROOM. PENRITH POLICE STATION

[*Two police surgeons – one a young man, doing all the work. We see* TOPLIS*'s naked body, torn tongue sticking out*]

YOUNG SURGEON: . . . I can't get his tongue back in.

[*The tired surgeon holds up a scalpel. The* YOUNG SURGEON *takes it, sympathetically*]

Well, he'll never talk now . . .

[RITCHIE *and* WOODHALL *enter and stand in the doorway.* WOODHALL *nods*]

Just finishing him off, sir.

202/4. INT. THAT WHITEHALL DINING ROOM. DAY

[*The* HIGH-RANKING *civilian is talking on the telephone to* WOODHALL *whilst drinking his port. His colleagues are on to the cigars*]

HIGH RANKING: Good . . . Good. Well, carry on.

[*He puts the telephone down and the flunky takes it away*]

Excellent inquest. All resolved. 'Justifiable killing'. And little Edwin is busy tidying up.

MELLOW: Did he – I mean, was Woodhall actually involved?

UNCIVILIZED: Don't think he'd have missed that – he'd have been there. Somewhere.

HIGH RANKING: Yes. Oh yes. Let us drink to the toe rags who preserve the very fabric of decent society.

[*Brandified laughter and 'here heres'*]

I'm sorry, have I said that before . . .?

203/4. EXT. CEMETERY GATES. DAY

[*A multitude of journalists and photographers, outside a cemetery, drifting away. After looking at a sign on the cemetery gates.*

'TOPLIS *funeral postponed till one o'clock. Coffin not ready.*'

ANNIE *and* MAM *are also there. They are the last to leave*]

204/4. EXT. POLICE YARD

[*We see a lorry with 'Bartley's Lemonade and Mineral Water' on it.*
We see FULTON *and three policemen hustling the coffin onto the lorry, furtively. We see the lorry rushing out of the police station, coffin bouncing*]

205/4. INT. CHAPEL. DAYTIME

[*We see a policeman enter the chapel, go to* FULTON *and nod that everything is ready. He takes his place by the coffin.*
RITCHIE, FULTON *and* BERTRAM *are inside the chapel with the coffin. We also see the* REVEREND LAW, *dressed to pray*]

FULTON: They've all gone now, sir.
RITCHIE: You don't have to say too much with this one, Reverend.
REVEREND LAW: Gentlemen, please, let us remember that the deceased has not been convicted of any capital crime. And I intend to conduct a proper service, as best I can. Circumstances have been such that this man was violently removed from this life before he could be judged on earth. Let his only judgement, therefore, be made in Heaven. Let us pray. I am the Resurrection and the light saith the Lord.

[*We return to the scene to see the four policemen. Straggling into song with* REVEREND LAW]

REVEREND LAW: There is a happy land. 1,2,3,4.
ALL OF THEM: There is a happy land, far far away . . .
Where Saints in glory stand, bright, bright as day.
Oh how they sweetly sing, worthy is our Saviour King,
Loud his praises sing, praise praise for aye.

Come to this happy land, come come away.
Why will ye doubting stand, why still delay?
Oh we shall happy be, when from sin and sorrow free,
Lord we shall live with thee, blest, blest for aye.

206/4. EXT. CEMETERY

[*By the mound of earth/graveside.* ANNIE *puts flowers on the grave and goes to* TOPLIS*'s mother in her wheelchair.*

Somewhere else, we see WOODHALL, *watching. He turns away.*

ANNIE *pushes* MAM *down the path. They pass* DOROTHY, *who goes to stand by the grave. Finally she turns away and goes down the path*]

FADE OUT